NOW I SEE

An Invitation to Life to the Full

Zach Elliott

with Rebecca Sandberg

Text copyright © 2019 by Zach Elliott and Rebecca Sandberg
Cover art by Rob Stainback and Rebecca Sandberg
Artwork copyright © 2019 by Rebecca Sandberg

For information about special bulk purchases, please contact
www.zachjelliott.com

Scripture quotations are taken from the Holy Bible, New Living
Translation, copyright ©1996, 2004, 2015 by Tyndale House
Foundation. Used by permission of Tyndale House Publishers, Inc.,
Carol Stream, Illinois 60188. All rights reserved.

Published in the United States by Lost Poet Press
First paperback edition.

www.zachjelliott.com
rebecca-sandberg.com
www.lostpoetpress.com

ISBN: 1-944470-06-9
ISBN-13: 978-1-944470-06-7

For Caminique, Bella, Holland,

Olivia, Jude, and Aurora.

The vision is Jesus.

May you know life to the full looking to Him,

like Him, and with Him.

Now and forever.

I love Him and I love you.

CONTENTS

FOREWORD

For I am about to do something new.
See, I have already begun! Do you not see it?
I will make a pathway through the wilderness.
I will create rivers in the dry wasteland.

Isaiah 43:19 NLT

I met Zach in an ice cream line at a social gathering about five years ago. My husband and I exchanged pleasantries with him and his wife, Cammie, while scooping vanilla, chocolate, and a helping of where-are-you-from small talk. We have been family friends ever since.

I remember several years ago, sitting at a table watching Zach eagerly scribble out the main premise of this message as he asked me to help him organize and edit his writings. He quite literally bounced and smiled as he explained the ideas that have become the book you now hold. He finished by writing these words: *the vision is Jesus* and then emphatically underlined it several times, tossed the pen on the table, and said it out loud again,

"The vision is Jesus!" He threw his arms up in a silent amen. Yes!

I gave a smile.

Duh. I know that. Jesus.

I wasn't thinking that in a patronizing way. It just didn't seem like a revolutionary idea.

I grew up in the church, as did Zach, well-versed in religion. But there was something altogether different about Zach, something light. He seemed to have a secret that I didn't know about. I had eaten religion for breakfast, lunch, and dinner. I read Berkhof's *Systematic Theology* when I was fifteen, twice, and pounded out most of Jonathan Edwards' *Religious Affections* prior to my senior year in college, among other things. By all academic and theological standards, the state of my soul should have been healthy.

I got it, but I didn't *have* it.

Trying to keep my soul afloat was exhausting, and I couldn't figure out why. I loved Jesus, but something was missing. I had no idea what it was, and no idea where to find it. My sense of flourishing was mostly circumstantial, though I would have emphatically staked my life on the argument that it was not. I lived in a mental and spiritual landscape of scarcity. Protect and survive. There is only so much to go around. Work hard and be kind. Get 'er done.

Zach said the words again, "The vision is Jesus!"

I smiled. "I love it! Great message. How can I help?"

With that I agreed to partner with Zach on this project, though I knew little at the time about how it would truly change my whole existence.

Zach has been developing the concepts in this book for over two decades, investing countless hours preaching, counseling, and teaching. I came into this as a rookie. Zach is to Yoda as I am to Luke. (Can we please say Leia instead? My hair looks better in side buns.) Everything that I thought I knew, I really didn't. As we delved into the heart of this project, Zach often repeated his mantra, *the vision is Jesus.* Uh-huh. Yup. Of course, it is. I continued editing and reading and doing rewrites. The vision is Jesus. I shook my head and nodded in agreement … until I didn't.

Do you really think so, Rebecca?

I shut that voice up quick. Of course, I knew the vision was Jesus!

The truth, I eventually came to discover, was that I was blind. By day, I tried to live *for* Christ as best I knew how, and *for* His kingdom to the best of my ability. But at night, I was alone, terrified and desperate to the point of literally not breathing. *I can't keep up. I can't breathe. I don't want to do this anymore.*

As this project began to come together, my inner and outer world began to come apart. Pain upon pain

3

unleashed. The default survival tactics of my soul were exposed as circumstance-triggered coping mechanisms. My marriage buckled, my identity bent, and my relationships got turned inside out. Through it all I nodded and smiled, but then quickly closed my mouth lest people see my teeth rattling like the hinges on an out-of-control train. If anyone actually saw me, they may have noticed the bolts of my brain flying away at the speed of sound, while my soul erupted like Mt. Saint Helens. The great ring of fire within me was awake. The tectonic plates shifted, the support beams bowed, and all the pretty dishes came crashing to the ground.

If all of this comes undone, I will have nothing left. I cannot and will not let my circumstances fall apart. I will outrun this. I did what I knew to do. I prayed. I cried. I read my Bible. But, without relationship, without seeing my Father, it was all just done in abstraction.

The idea I lived by was to "believe". You must believe. I believed in God the Father. I believed in the resurrection and the communion of saints. I prayed for God to forgive me for what I had done and what I had left undone. You can be sure that I recited the Nicene Creed more times than I even care to count. *I believed!*

In the midst of it all, Zach wouldn't leave me alone.

He would say things like, "Look up at the Milky Way!" or "Go outside and grab some dirt."

4

"What? Seriously?" Zach says some odd things. "I can't look at the Milky Way right now. I am running around holding up the universe. Ahem. I have some things going on."

Nevertheless, as Zach does, he brought what he had. He sent me emails and audio clips and articles and testimonials and chapter after chapter of this book to edit and organize. As I did, Zach's words and the invitation of this book revealed a path I had not seen before. Every chapter of this book is a vantage point of something spectacular, a destination in and of itself, a place to stop and see anew the message of the gospel.

Viewpoint after viewpoint, always with the vision as Jesus. One step at a time, until you loop back all the way to the beginning and do the journey over and over and over again.

In the midst of writing and typing and ordering all of these words, the *true* words of this book loosened the untrue words of my life. Anger and tears, shock and awe, guttural sobs and giddy laughter, chapter after chapter until one day, not too many months ago, I saw something new. Like Celidonius, a man you will meet in the pages of this book, I felt the face of Jesus, scarred and marred and disfigured. I locked eyes with Him, and I heard His voice call me *beloved,* and nothing will ever be the same.

Circumstances the same? Probably.

Vision the same? No.

The embrace of the Father changes everything. Once that relationship is set right, we remember who we *actually* are, and everything is made new. As Jesus claims in the scriptures, He came that we might have life to the full.[1]

The message of this book saved my life. I was in a nightmare, asleep on the side of the road. Zach patiently said, "Wake up, oh sleeper, my sister, *wake up*." Zach reminded me of my true identity, something so far back on the shelves of my mind that it took a while for me to find it again, tucked in a folder on the top shelf of my childhood, a bright red heart that simply said: *Jesus loves you*.

Zach doesn't peddle religion. He is a man close to Jesus. When I met Zach in that ice cream line years ago, I didn't think that Jesus was there too. But He was. And He knew what was ahead. I look back now and I see Jesus standing right there with His healing and gentle hands on my shoulders and His marvelous eyes of love piercing my soul. I had no idea.

This book is an invitation to see the Father, the Savior, the King. It is not a book to tell you what to do, but an invitation to a relationship. In some ways, I see it as a field manual for spiritual life.

Zach and Cammie have walked alongside countless people, loving them like Jesus, replacing lies with Truth, and inviting people to life to the full. Not because they have it all together, but because they have seen the King. It has been a privilege to live this message out in community with them, in celebration of the good, in gut-wrenching brokenness, and in sheer laughter and awe at the future. Our families have shared birthdays, breakdowns, breakfasts, hikes, holidays, worship, and true fellowship. Life together.

When we see Jesus, everything changes. Where despair has overtaken us, we will celebrate the good. Where indifference has restricted us, we will affirm the broken and mourn with those who mourn. Where apathy has arrested us, we will instead hope in a future and participate in love. The vision is Jesus. Look to Him, look like Him, and look with Him, over and over again.

Come and see.

Rebecca Sandberg

A Note from the Author

Dear Reader,

The journey you are about to go on with me is simply a story ... my story. The trail guide imagery is the metaphor I found to communicate my discovery of life to the full. I am not a scholar, not a theologian, not a professor. I am just an ordinary man who knows Jesus and longs to experience and share life together in Him.

This is a story, and yet it is not the whole story. This is a map, but it does not contain the whole landscape. It would be impossible to combine every important doctrinal perspective or spiritual discipline into one book, and that is not the purpose of this one. The purpose is to invite you to look to Jesus, to see Him, and to know Him. In relationship with Him, all truth becomes evident. Out of relationship with Him, all truth becomes warped.

My story is a thread, woven into the seams of the wholeness that is to come.

I invite you to add the thread of your own story.

Together, I believe we will discover more life and beauty than we have ever dreamed possible.

The Vision is Jesus.

Zach Elliott

Life to the full is a mystery and a miracle.

Nothing less.

You are invited.

May this story be *your* story.

PROLOGUE

The Invitation

The glory of God is man fully alive.

St. Irenaeus

I'll never forget the first day I sat down to write this book. I was seated at the Oxford Exchange in downtown Tampa, Florida. In the 1800s, this building began as a stable in a small town known for cigars and trade. As Tampa grew, the Oxford Exchange evolved into one of the most popular gathering places for hipsters and executives alike, housing a menagerie of eateries, trendy shops, and communal office spaces. The unique and luxurious architecture creates an invigorating vibe that cultivates community, conversation, connection, and creativity.

I love the Oxford Exchange. There is life and beauty there, a deep heritage rich with story and culture. I remember writing that day, watching the sunbeams dance on the floor by the station of a man shining shoes, and noticing the people that moved purposefully through the building. For a moment, I saw the good.

But I also saw something else that day.

Something was off. Something was missing.

In a place filled with such success and luxury and an atmosphere of the good life, one would expect to see something *alive* in people: energy, joy, and flourishing. Instead, I saw a void, a sadness, and a profound exhaustion. I saw loneliness on the faces of people who were surrounded by what seemingly could have helped them feel full and connected. I saw something broken.

And yet, the brokenness wasn't all that I saw that day. As I ebbed between writing, observing, thinking, and noticing, I glimpsed a vision of something different. Something deeper. Something *more* real than the beautiful architecture, something *more* true than the weary clientele. The vision came from a place beyond the scope of my physical sight, born out of a journey towards Love that has now changed everything about the way I see. The vision filled my soul with the electric anticipation of hope and compelled me to tell this story.

I glimpsed a vision of shalom.

Shalom

An examination of every culture and religion throughout

11

history would reveal attempts to achieve some version of life to the full. Words like shalom, flourishing, peace, and zen are used at liberty these days. They are not new concepts. They have been recycled, used in both sacred and secular ways to describe what humans long for.

Shalom is originally a religious term. The writers of the Old Testament used the word shalom to describe a life of wholeness and peace.[2] It is when the soul finally breathes. Yes! A wonderful, rich word with ancient threads. Religion claims to offer shalom. Religion says, "We have an answer! It's right here. Sing these songs, read these texts, obey this God, be a part of this community, and your life will change!" We are experts at religion. *But if those things could give us shalom, then wouldn't we have it by now?*

We *get* it, but we don't *have* it.

So, we look beyond religion. We work tirelessly, study diligently, adventure wildly, and spend extravagantly to try to secure a sense of flourishing. All of this effort yields some sort of temporary satisfaction, but it is not fulfilling. This false flourishing is actually a *withering.* We feel it when we stop to think for a minute … or maybe that's why we don't stop.

I am a pastor. I would like to tell you that it's different in my world. I would like to tell you that I don't see the lifeless and exhausted expressions on the faces of people who claim to have found God, but I can't. The church is not immune. This reality breaks my heart. It keeps me up at night, wrestling with the pain of watching fellow believers just surviving, barely breathing.

Is it possible that our perception of the Christian life is incorrect? Is it possible that flourishing and authentic relationship with a loving God are actually available to us? Is it possible that we don't have to feel so disenchanted and exhausted and afraid anymore?

It is possible. But only in a way of life that starts at the source: Jesus. Don't tune me out just yet. I know that sounds precisely like the Christian life you've heard about a million times before. But remember this distinction: *we get it, but we don't have it.* Stay with me here, because there is something important to discover in the pages of this book. I am writing to you about the story we were actually created for, something true and beautiful and real. No more emptiness or loneliness. No more exhaustion or hopelessness. This is an invitation to life to the full.

The Vision is Jesus

My story of discovering life to the full begins in a place where I never wanted to be.

I never planned to be a pastor; in fact, I wanted to be a pirate. Since my parents didn't agree with my career choice, my first job as a young man was selling flowers as part of my very own business venture. It was a character-building experience to say the least, but I outgrew it and ended up getting a job as a forensic evidence technician for the Oregon State Police. I loved law enforcement, but it was heartbreaking. I ended up back in business, another venture, pursuing wealth and living the good life. One day, my brother-in-law asked me to come to his church to talk to their youth group about not doing drugs. I said yes as a favor to him. It was never my intention to make a vocation out of anything spiritual.

In those days, I believed in the truth of the gospel, but there was a problem that haunted me and kept me running all the time. *I was broken.* I had done things and left things undone that I shouldn't have. The layers of shame were making me sweat, but I couldn't take them off. I was a broken man in a broken world, feeling like I was watching everything go to hell. I didn't want to hurt like that anymore. I fought against it for years by pursuing any sort of pleasure or relief I could find.

The story of the gospel is a story of hope, but it became harder and harder for me to reconcile the injustice and brokenness I witnessed in my law enforcement days and in my own life with this story of Jesus. My question came down to this: *is this story true, or isn't it?* It can't be partly true. If God is who He says He is, then it is 100% true. If He isn't who He says He is, then the whole thing is false, and hope is dead.

I reached a point in my life where I chose to hope again. I finally chose to surrender to this story of Jesus, and to allow the transformation of my soul. I had come to the end of myself, so I determined to give this Jesus life everything that was left of me, and to believe in His claims of redemption. For a while I felt a sense of flourishing, and it catapulted me onto a path of becoming a pastor.

But that was not the end of the story.

A year into pastoring, I was disillusioned and heartbroken. I observed the Church and its programs and practices. I watched the rhythms of its people. Where was the hope? Where was the sense of shalom? I didn't see radical love coming alive within us. I didn't see flourishing. I was stuck managing people and programs and felt like I was slowly *dying*. Worse, I was complicit in advancing the mess.

The sheer angst pushed me to a defining moment, as angst will often do. I was deeply frustrated. I wanted to see the gospel come to life within me and around me. One day, I went into my office and shut my door, ready to tell God I was done. A long, unnerving silence settled in the room. I was unable to say what I wanted to say. And then … a still, small voice. His Voice.

Without vision, the people perish.[3]

It felt trite at first. What vision? What vision

15

could be enough to kindle a true sense of hope and peace and life and beauty? There was a vision statement on the wall of my church that was a good sentiment, but it certainly wasn't enough to keep us alive.

Without vision, the people perish.

I knew there was something important here. I began to think about the word "vision". I heard echoes from my childhood, of songs like "Be Thou my Vision" and "Jesus, Be the Center". I thought of my adolescent years reading Bonhoeffer's *Christ the Center*. And then I remembered a line from a poem by Pete Greig[4] that my mom once shared with me.

The Vision is Jesus.

Over and over again, these words bounced in my mind like fireflies in a jar. I grabbed four blank sheets of paper and put them next to each other on my desk. I wrote these simple scrawls, one on each page:

Vision Up
Vision In
Vision Out
The Vision is Jesus

When I put my pen down, I felt like I had just come up from deep beneath the surface of the ocean. I was gasping the air that was finally there to breathe. I felt alive. Slowly, this vision began to change everything about my life: my heart, my work, and my church. I began to see the right order of things and discovered the cycle of experiencing life to the full, the true transformation that occurs when our vision is actually Jesus Himself. And then, after years of doubt and disenchantment, I began to see glimpses of shalom. My circumstances had not changed. My perception and my vision had changed, and thus, so had my life. I began to develop a deep longing to live this way and to share this truth with people.

And so, this book was born. On napkins and legal pads, in voice recordings and long conversations, the truth of the gospel came alive in this framework. Though I have found myself lost along this trail at different times, and though I still struggle and have much to learn and discover, I have truly experienced a transition from withering to flourishing. That day in my office was fourteen years ago now. I have lived and breathed and taught on the principals of VU, VI, and VO to many people over the years, traversing this path and seeing the life and beauty it holds for all of us. I want to present you with a trail guide of sorts that will take us on a journey to look at flourishing from a different viewpoint.

The vision is Jesus.

The promise is life to the full.

Life to the Full

These four words are the invitation of this book. It promises a shift in perspective, new vision to see first and foremost who Jesus is, and then phenomenally and profoundly who you truly are. I'll be honest. It's risky. But it is what your weary soul is longing for. I want this for my wife and my four growing children, my neighbors near or far, for myself, and for you. I want us to be brave and genuine. I want us to disconnect from all of the lesser sources and connect to the One who literally breathes life into creation. I want us to breathe that life anew.

Perhaps in this moment, you are curious enough to read on. Perhaps with this glimpse of where we are, you are ready to hear about where the journey might lead. The Creator of the universe is calling. The source of Perfect Love longs for you to receive it.

Are you ready to see?
Then come with me.
But be brave. Oh, be brave!

The first thing we see is the darkness.

Section One

The Cave

Darkness

Suffocating. Stale.
It is dark here,
But the dark is all I know.
God is dead.
Religion is dead.
I am alone in the center,
Longing for Another.

Hearing

It hurts.
This loneliness is killing me.
I must numb it or silence it.
Curse the ones who speak of hope.
There is no hope save the hope I make.
Somehow, I will soothe my ache.
But that sound? There again.
Faint, but I hear it.
Something is with me.
I am…
Uneasy.

Awakening

An ember kindled with a whisper.
Strange.
Beautiful.
I will not put it down.
I am afraid, but awake.
The Voice will not leave now.
I don't want it to.
It calls me
Beloved.

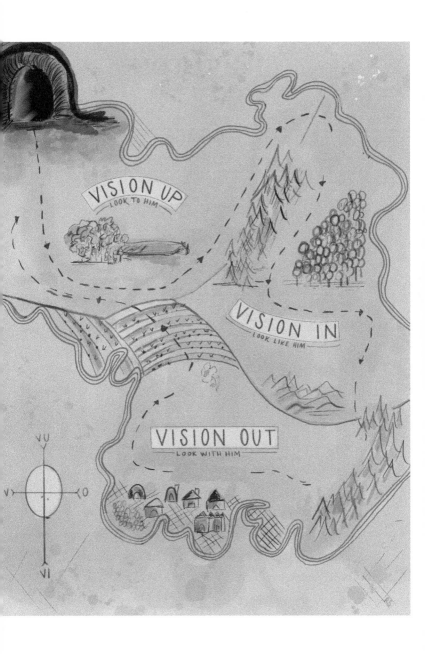

CHAPTER ONE

Darkness

It cannot be seen, cannot be felt,
cannot be heard, cannot be smelt.
It lies behind stars and under hills,
and empty holes it fills.
It comes first and follows after,
ends life, kills laughter.

J.R.R. Tolkien, on darkness

The wind blows, and the clap of the leaves echoes in the distance. If I were standing with you, you would see that I am taking a deep breath. I want to take you on a journey along this trail towards life to the full. I hope that as the story unfolds in the pages of this book, you will hear an invitation to flourishing and relationship. But before we begin, we must take stock of where we are. My older brother reminds me that the way down can often lead to the way up.[5] *Up* is where we are headed: Vision

Up. But our pursuit of looking up begins by looking down into the darkness of a cave.

We are about to go on a brief dive into Nietzsche and Plato and several other scholars and philosophers, past and present. We will look at their contributions to this conversation, because it is an age-old discussion. These questions have been asked before. My hope is that as we join this conversation, we will locate ourselves in a larger context. We will see the chapters of our own stories as part of a whole, and in doing so we will hear the invitation to where we might travel.

A Flattened Age

We live in what philosopher Charles Taylor describes as a flattened and disenchanted age,[6] a way of life lived without a transcendent view. Places with high ceilings draw the eyes and attention up, like libraries, cathedrals, or auditoriums, and they evoke feelings of space and freedom. Places with low ceilings, where it's possible to bump your head on the door or scrape your hair on the ceiling, evoke something like claustrophobia. In these places we can feel limited, enclosed, or even anxious.

The "ceiling" of our modern age has slowly lowered to the point that we feel it now. It presses down on our necks and compresses our breath. We live under this flattened ceiling. It is where we work, play, and even worship. Beneath it, we are restless. What flattened our modern age? What lowered the ceiling?

We killed the Creator.

We declared God dead, erased Him from the story and believed wholeheartedly that this idea would liberate us. Nietzsche's well-known quote, "God is dead", often excludes the whole of his sentimental and prophetic statement:

> "God is dead. God remains dead. And we have killed him. How shall we comfort ourselves, the murderers of all murderers…what water is there for us to clean ourselves? What festivals of atonement, what sacred games shall we have to invent…Must we ourselves not become gods simply to appear worthy of it?"

When we declared God dead, we could no longer claim that we came from somewhere. We lost our relationship, and therefore our identity. We accepted the story that we are alone, and at the center of reality. We built our modern age on this not-so-new paradigm, and it has led to a disdain for anything that resembles God. Without a Creator to anchor our original story, we continue to experience an utter loss of identity.

God is dead. We ultimately declare this in politics, education, the social sector, business, and sometimes even religion. If God is no longer at the center of reality, with us orbiting around him, then as Nietzsche said, "Must we ourselves not become gods simply to appear worthy?" Without God in the center, we collectively stepped in and claimed it for ourselves. We are now alone and in the center, with no way of knowing our bearings. The ceiling of our age collapses around us, flattening our reality into something we were never created to participate in.

Alone and in the Center

I used to buy into this way of thinking. I used to believe that I could experience a full and flourishing life by standing proudly – and alone – at the center of my own existence. I didn't see the flattening of my reality until it was almost too late to escape.

When I was a kid, I used to spend hours looking through my dad's record collection. From John Lennon to Elton John, from the Beach Boys to the Oakridge Boys, it was all magical. I loved to bring the music to life through an old, Pioneer amplifier and wood-cased speakers that sat on the floor next to our makeshift entertainment center. The real magic, the power, was actually in the loudness button on the front of the amplifier. Pushing that button opened the door to a completely different world of sound. It was full and clear. You could feel the tones separate and swell, working in concert. When the loudness button was disengaged, the magic was gone. I could still hear the music, but I felt separated from it, almost like it had been cut in half. It was no longer full; it was compressed, muted, and flat.

In my early twenties, that's how my *life* felt. No matter how full my days or rich my experiences, I felt contained, flattened, and trapped. I felt like I needed to clear my ears in order to hear, or climb above some mountain so that I could get a full view. But the more I tried, the less I heard and the less I saw. At first, it was the slightest feeling of separation, a subtle and internal withdrawal. Externally, no one would ever have noticed. I was still present and did my best to be the version of myself that everyone knew. But inside was a different story. Slowly, over time, internal separation and withdrawal became my way. Even when I was present, the deep parts of me were not. My ceiling was compressing. I was drifting to a space where I was alone and in the center of my existence.

My law enforcement days solidified the flattening. I remember the day the ceiling pushed me so low that I thought I might be trapped forever. I was taking pictures at a crime scene where someone was killed, and I had a transcendent moment. I was fully present as I photographed the scene; the loudness button was *on*. I felt disturbed but awake in the contrast of life and death.

It was later that night when I got home that I knew something was wrong. After walking the long entry hall to the kitchen, I set my keys on the table and stood there, watching the headlights pass on the street below. Other than the faint sound of evening traffic on the wet pavement, it was quiet. Minutes went by before I finally found my way to the couch and sat down. I rested my head on my hands and stared at the rusted, iron pull on the armoire. I began to be aware of a deep sadness within me. I couldn't trace it to any specific source, and it wasn't attached to what I had experienced that day.

It was what I had found at home.

Right there, in the center of my apartment, I was empty. I was alone. I couldn't find the loudness button inside. I couldn't flip the switch and feel the layers of reality and life around me. Everything felt flat, compressed, and oh so lonely.

This idea that we are intended to be at the center of everything has stolen our life and beauty. Where we once knew enchantment and relationship, we now find disillusionment and isolation. This flattened age bears down on us. Our story is troubled and disturbed. We feel it. Beneath this ceiling, the thing we long for is God himself, Immanuel. The creature within us is longing to return home and embrace the Creator. That's what we were created for, but we have rejected that story, rejected the idea that such a relationship can truly exist. Many of us who call ourselves Christians have thrown out the story that includes a personal, thriving, tangible relationship with a living God.

The truth is that the story does exist, and we are characters in it. There is something about us that was written from the beginning and extends into the fullness of the whole story, one in which *God is alive*. The rest of the story, the part we took out when we accepted God's death, is the mystery. Charles Taylor affirms that the part we took out is haunted by something "Other,"[8] that there is something that calls to us from above the flattened ceiling of our existence. The Spirit of God hovers above creation, above that ceiling, longing to restore relationship as it was intended. We feel the longing for it, we sense the haunting of it, and we are restless. Of course we are.

That day in my apartment, alone and in the center, I realized I was withering. My light was growing dim. How could it be that being around *death* was what had actually made me feel *alive* that day? Darkness was stealing light within the spaces of my soul, shaping me to be a creature more comfortable in the dark. I was adapting to the flattened space, losing any conception of a Creator and drifting into isolation.

I have seen this story too often repeated in the lives of those around me. How have we gotten here? And why can't we escape? Perhaps an ancient allegory can help us make sense of it all.

The Allegory of the Cave

I first became aware of Plato's Allegory of the Cave[9] many years ago when I was in school. This metaphor helps us locate ourselves on the trail as we begin our journey. I invite you to examine the cave with me. This cave is where I found myself that day in my apartment, and it is the place so many of us have been imprisoned.

Imagine a cave, deep underground, where a row of people stands shackled. A fire dances a short distance behind them and casts its light on their backs, while shadows are projected on the wall in front of them. The captives can only see the shadows cast on the wall, nothing else. They have never been outside of the cave to experience the true reality of light and life. Consequently, they believe that the shadow reality is, in fact, the only reality that exists at all.

Imagine that we are prisoners in this cave. The darkness and shadow reality play tricks on our eyes and our hearts. The air is thin, the light is dim, and as Nietzsche predicted, we are sad. We are alive, and outwardly all seems well, but in truth we are empty and numb. Our gaunt souls are like sacks of skin with nothing to hold them up. Those shadows on the wall are designed to keep us here. They offer familiarity and false comfort. They make sense in the dark of the cave, so we remain imprisoned. We stay in the comfort of what we know rather than risk exposure to what we cannot comprehend.

What if someone, as Plato suggests, were pulled from the cave? Imagine both the wonder and difficulty of seeing an entirely new landscape, rich with depth and full of color. Memories of life in the cave would provoke a range of emotions. And if the freed captive returned to challenge the narrative of the cave? The allegory suggests that light entering the darkness would so threaten the captives that the one who dared to return would be mocked, marginalized, and ridiculed. Maybe even killed.

And here we are.

And *that we did.*

We killed God, declared him dead, and anchored ourselves in the cave.

Perfect Love entered the cave and spoke Truth, and we killed Perfect Love. This spawned a Copernican-like revolution, creating a totally different system where everything orbits not around the Creator but around us, the new gods. From our dim and distorted viewpoint, we are unable to see how deeply our society has suffered harm. Our souls have been individually and collectively devastated by this God-is-dead narrative.

In this state, we do not want the truth. We wake up in the morning and our first unspoken exhale of the day is, "I would rather be a god in here than be a creature out there." The same deceitful voice that Adam and Eve heard at the beginning of time still invites us to be our own god. And so, we listen to the voice of the cave. The whisper to our egos puffs us up and strokes our desperate souls. The lie of the cave is that we can be gods … but the truth is, that's exhausting, and incredibly lonely.

The story on the wall of the cave runs in a loop. And we are spellbound. Flattened fiction over and over again. We are sad, yet in the center. We are enslaved, yet entertained. We exist under a ceiling that stifles our freedom, yet we are comfortable because we have become acclimated to our captivity. This cave narrative demands a way of life that is *so far from our reason for being*.

Flourishing

We long to flourish. We long for life to the full. So, what has gone wrong, and how can we find our way out of this cave?

Here's the issue: we made the starting point *circumstance*. We believed that our circumstance would and could save us, that it would and could be the defining factor of our flourishing. The trajectory of this idea is catastrophic and heartbreaking. Our cave fiction has taught us to believe that favorable circumstances--the accumulation of wealth, relationships, networks, success and experiences--are what it means to flourish.

Friends, the starting point is not a circumstance; it is a Person. Flourishing is relational, *not* circumstantial.

The invitation of this book is an invitation to know the Creator and experience Perfect Love; it is not a guidebook for how to shift your circumstance. No possession, change of scenery, or alteration of circumstance can fill what is lacking.[10] The starting point is relationship, and the trajectory of this idea is life to the full.

In the cave, we take on the sole responsibility to create flourishing and shalom. But that is not our purpose, nor were we created with the ability to do so. We cannot manufacture the fulfillment of our own lives; that can only be found in relationship with the Creator. Our lives have been designed to experience peace, the place where the soul breathes, the true definition of shalom.

The good news is that the illusion within the cave can be exposed, if we choose to hear.

The darkness of the cave can actually *serve* us. It can teach us to listen. The cave is haunted by a Voice that echoes through the chamber, whispering, calling, always present and always speaking. It is a gentle Voice with a strange authority that speaks directly to our soul, deep calling to deep. Listen. It awakens us. The One we were made by and for has been speaking since the beginning, creating and calling, illuminating and guiding. This Voice sets captives free and gives sight to the blind.

We hear before we see.

CHAPTER TWO

Hearing

If I find in myself desires which
nothing in this world can satisfy,
the only logical explanation
is that I was made for another world.

C.S. Lewis

The still, small Voice echoes somewhere beyond the scope of our sight.

A couple of years ago, I had a conversation with a research analyst regarding the radiation leak in Fukushima. We were talking about the impact that the radiation would have on the ocean in the Pacific Northwest. He told me that radiation in the ocean is a valid concern, but that a far greater concern is the radiation that enters the atmosphere every time we test or detonate a nuclear bomb. The radiation stays; it takes years to diminish. It enters the dirt, the air, the water we drink, the food we eat, and the atmosphere of our beautiful planet. It accumulates there, particle upon particle.

The Truth is like that. It's radioactive in that sense. It fills the atmosphere, particle upon particle. Every time someone or something testifies to the Truth, the particles collect. And yet in the cave, although we are aware of their presence, we cannot *see* them; we cannot see the Truth. We do our best in the cave and sometimes, for brief moments, we hear those Truth particles vibrating, mingling, colliding, collecting – they are there, present somehow. In these thin moments and thin places, we know that *something else* is with us in the cave.

One of the most transformational particle-swirling moments for me happened on the island of Oahu. Everything in my life had begun to feel meaningless, flat, and empty. I had searched for community in law enforcement, in the church, and among friends. Nothing could satisfy me. I had become restless, which for me looked like running, exhaustion, disappointment, anger, regret, and despair. So, I ran as far west as I could, and when that didn't work, I hopped on a plane and kept going until I landed in Hawaii.

That is how I ended up on the North Shore of Oahu, drunk and alone.

I buried my feet in the warm sand, and with the help of the alcohol I was lulled into thinking I had finally outrun the restlessness. For a brief moment I thought the shadow broke. The mystery and vastness pierced my drunken fog. I was drawn to look up, and I stared up at the sky. I wished I could stay right there forever.

And then something happened. There was no voice, no vision; it was just a haunted moment. Particles of truth gently brushed the top of my soul like snow, making me look up to find where they were coming from. That's when the chill came. It wasn't snow; it was Truth. As I looked up at the moon and stars, I realized that I was very much *not alone*.

Haunted

Do you hear it? The Voice of the One we called dead actually whispers to us in the cave. It's a haunting whisper that beckons us, a murmur that unsettles us, a song we ache to hum along with ... if only we could remember the tune. That Voice echoes in the order and beauty of nature, the kindness of a stranger, peace in the dark, and the warmth of the light. We witness traces of beauty and hope that sound like something very different than the flattened noise of the cave.

Charles Taylor and J.K. Smith have done a powerful job giving us this visual.[11] The cave is quite literally an echo chamber, a constant barrage of recycled imagery proclaiming this fiction that has become our codified, sacred belief. But the cave also echoes with the still, small Voice of the One who calls us. We know the cave is haunted. We can feel it. Martyrs and prophets, preachers and poets, artists and scholars and most often children have all pointed towards the sound of this haunting Voice, even if they have not clearly seen its source.

Those of us who are dwelling in this cave hear the faint, quiet whisper. That's what makes us *uneasy*. But we cannot see where it's coming from, and we cannot understand it. Truth doesn't feel real, because we are convinced that the flattened fiction we have come to believe and accept is more real than Truth. We reject the idea that anything beyond the cave exists. We are so distracted that we don't hear the haunting Voice that speaks of freedom.

Or perhaps we try. Perhaps we try this God thing, or as close to a god thing as we can imagine from within the cave. Perhaps we go to church, say the prayers, and make the confessions. Perhaps we show up, serve, and give faithfully but then realize we have nothing to show for it, no transformation or growth of any kind, and often a load of shame and guilt. The god we encounter in the cave seems just as empty and meaningless as anything else, because the god we encounter in the cave is nothing but a creation of our own imagination. And so, ironically, the whispering echo and promise of life to the full becomes the haunting thing that so many of us choose to ignore.

This cave life is not the way it is supposed to be.[12] Creation was made to flourish, made for life and beauty in relationship. God has never stopped speaking since the moment of creation, entering the darkness to set us free and bring us back into right relationship with Him. He moves and speaks in the cave, through His Spirit, in dreams, in visions, in convictions, through His creation, through His messengers, and through His still, small Voice. His aim is always to set things right and bring us back to the source of all life and beauty.

The Real Problem

There is a deep pain present within all who live in the cave: loneliness.

We were not created to be alone.

Though a mass of humanity surrounds us, and a vast array of technology connects us, we are so sad and so alone in the cave. It hurts more than we dare to admit. We almost feel like we can't be honest about it, because there has never been a time in history when humanity has been more "connected". Social media likes and followers and friends are our measuring sticks for successful relationships, and so we expand our platforms and our networks in an effort to combat our loneliness. This connectivity is a smoke screen. A red herring. There remains a deep and severe ache within our souls for connection, for relationship. And this false connectedness will only deepen as technological invention increases.

The darkest lie of the cave is this: *the lonely ache can be soothed in here.*

And so, we search for the antidote to our intense feelings of isolation. When our needs can't be met, they must be mitigated. We turn to external relationships that promise connection: family, spouses, children, friends, co-workers, partners, communities ... but if we are not connected to the source, this only provides temporary relief to our loneliness. We turn to activities that promise fulfillment: success, achievement, creative pursuits, acquiring wealth ... but enough is never enough. We turn to institutions that promise guidance: church, government, education, medicine... but it all feels like more of the same nothingness. We turn to the practices that promise help: counseling, yoga, books, therapies, retreats, coaching ... but none of it gets to the bottom of our pain. Much of this is good, but none of it can fill the void that is craving the connection we were created for.

We exhaust ourselves searching the cave for the answer to our loneliness. We are spent. We grope in the dark with blinded eyes, trying to heal the pain or satisfy the longing, but we can see nothing else to turn to. Quietly and reluctantly, we start to accept the loneliness. It hurts. So we medicate it, or seek pleasure, or run. Maybe the saddest move is when we just *survive it.* We begin to accept and believe that the loneliness is the sickness of our souls, and we will carry it forever. There is no cure. There is no healing. There is no Healer.

Our heads fall forward and our lungs constrict. We try to plug our ears. And yet we hear the haunting Voice again, as soft as a feather. It is the promise of healing, a whisper that maybe the pain can be alleviated by something we haven't yet found. Maybe it could be true that the answer to our pain and loneliness is actually something that we cannot see in this cave. But this time, we are at the end of ourselves, and we are frustrated and weary and desperate.

In this place of desperate loneliness, that haunting Voice might elicit *anger*. How dare anything or anyone ask us to get our hopes up again? We have numbed our pain well enough, and *we will not be fooled one more time into thinking there is a cure*. We can survive, medicated and numbed. Our life might not be full, but we will never again take the risk to believe that there is something more. That would be stupid and seriously naïve. In this place, the Voice of Truth sounds like the darkest of lies. We cannot possibly try any harder. We cannot possibly search any more.

That anger is a very real thing, and it can be a very good thing. Anger is like a fever. It alerts us that something is amiss. When I let the fever of anger go on and on and it turns into the septic flow of bitterness, it hurts others, and it hurts me. On the flip side, when I let the fever of anger lead me to awareness and truth, it invariably takes me to a place of *wonder*. I wonder, what is going on here? Is there something beyond what I can see? Why are my emotions so riled again by this thing I have chosen to believe does not exist? *What if...*

Our spines tingle with the electric current of something we cannot explain and cannot ignore, the sound of the God who was dead, somehow alive. And we are afraid. Oh yes, there is a great deal of fear present in these moments of wonder, because to acknowledge the Voice is also to acknowledge our loneliness, and it hurts more than anything.

This is what it is like to be haunted. It is unsettling, as it pokes our anger and flares up our fear. It is painful. But perhaps it is the very thing we need to lean into, and explore, and engage. Anger is our reaction to feeling trapped in isolation. Wonder has the power to set us free. The fact that we are unsettled is not a reminder that we are alone in the cave; it is evidence that we are not.

What was that?

The fact that we are unsettled is not a reminder that we are alone in the cave; it is evidence that we are not.

What if we allow this Voice to speak to us? Instead of running from it, or fighting it, or reasoning it away, or drowning it out with the immensity of other noises reverberating around us, what if we choose to listen?

We Hear Before We See

Something powerful happens when one of our senses is incapacitated: our other senses take over. When we stop adjusting our eyes to the lesser light and realize we are blind to true reality, then and only then can we hear more clearly. In this state of blindness, we can dare to listen.

Why didn't we hear this before? Maybe we did, but we rushed past it. Or we just attributed it to other things, or we were too distracted to notice. This is the game in the cave. Perhaps the immediacy of our circumstances demanded our attention. Perhaps we followed something that sounded similar and yet led us to another dead end.

But now we hear it. We close our eyes, we shut out the false narrative of the cave, and we hear the sound that we have always longed to hear, in the deepest and most raw places of our hearts and souls. We hear our name: *beloved*. We hear a gentle Voice calling us "child", the tender and merciful Voice of a Father calling us sons and daughters. This Voice has always been speaking and is always speaking.

Now, we are more afraid. This Voice is everything we have ever hoped for, which makes it the most terrifying thing we have ever heard. Could it be real? The particles of truth swirl around us now, their sound radiating in our cores. We are suddenly very much not alone, and we do not know for sure if that is the worst news or the best news of our lives.

Beloved.

We are restless. We are longing. We are afraid. But now we are listening.

In the 9th chapter of John's gospel we read about a blind man, who some early scholars have called Celidonius.[13] His sense of sight was gone, which allowed his ears to be acutely tuned to the sounds of the city. He recognized the voices that said the same thing in the same way, every day until one day an altogether different voice spoke, and Celidonius heard something new. Through all the noise of the familiar, Celidonius heard a still small Voice that spoke to him with authority, power, and beauty that resonated in a deeper frequency of the soul. He knew there was something different and life-altering in this Voice, and he chose to engage it, to trust it, to be transformed by it. He chose to listen, and because of that, he was given the gift of sight.

> *Then he [Jesus] spit on the ground, made mud with the saliva, and spread the mud over the blind man's eyes. He told him, "Go wash yourself in the pool of Siloam" (Siloam means "sent"). So the man went and washed and came back seeing!*

His neighbors and others who knew him as a blind beggar asked each other, "Isn't this the man who used to sit and beg?" Some said he was, and others said, "No, he just looks like him!"

But the beggar kept saying, "Yes, I am the same one!"

They asked, "Who healed you? What happened?"

He told them, "The man they call Jesus made mud and spread it over my eyes and told me, 'Go to the pool of Siloam and wash yourself.' So I went and washed, and now I can see!"

The villagers don't believe his tale, so they take him to the Pharisees, who question how and why this man Jesus would dare to heal on the Sabbath. Celidonius doesn't get caught up in their legalism or their doubt. He says simply this:

"But I know this: I was blind, and now I can see!"

Celidonius continues to argue with the Pharisees until they finally throw him out.

When Jesus heard what had happened, he found the man and asked, "Do you believe in the Son of Man?"

The man answered, "Who is he, sir? I want to believe in him."

"You have seen him," Jesus said, "and he is speaking to you!"

"Yes, Lord, I believe!" the man said. And he

worshiped Jesus.[14]

Our journey is similar to Celidonius'. Jesus' Voice calls to our deepest places, clearly and powerfully offering to heal our loneliness with his love. We must be willing to hear before we see. As we let the testimony of all creation lead us through a sea of idols, past the gods of our imagination who were birthed in our hearts and fashioned by our minds in the cave, we let the haunting Voice lead us to the only living God who speaks.

The Voice

The Voice of God echoes throughout all of creation. He is speaking to the deep loneliness within us. He resonates with our longings and awakens them within us. How could we not recognize His Voice? Just as a parent speaks to their unborn child in the womb, the Father spoke to us. We heard His Voice when He was creating us and knitting us together. He spoke to us then and He speaks to us now. It's His Voice calling, begging us to return, to come home to His presence, inviting us to flourish in the fullness of the life for which He created us.

Union with the Creator: that is what we're searching for. That is the only thing that will bring relief to the loneliness and peace to the anger. That is the only thing that will allow us to flourish. Until we hear, we will remain restless and we will wither because of it. This is the paradigm that must shift if we are to find our way out of the cave.

We are enticed, educated, and rewarded to accept the story in the cave. If we challenge the cave-narrative we are often mocked, shamed, and marginalized. So we come this far, hear the Truth, look up to find it … and then become lulled once again by the noise of the cave before we have a chance to fully see Him. The cycle continues. We return to the life of the cave, sad. We remain haunted, all the while becoming complicit in handing the flattened fiction and captivity down to the next generation.

Oh, but what if we didn't? What if we let our souls hum along to the song we can almost hear? What if we close our eyes to the false light and listen to the whisper on the wind? What if we lean headlong into the tension of fear and hope, of doubt and wonder, long enough to *awaken*?

CHAPTER THREE

Awakening

Awake my soul,
Awake my soul,
Awake my soul,
For you were made to meet your maker.

Mumford and Sons

Somewhere in between the moment that we hear and the moment that we see, we experience an *awakening*. If we do not have the experience of a new consciousness coming to life within us, we will eventually find ourselves lulled back to sleep by the din of the cave.

When we hear the haunting Voice, a spiritual dimension is awakened within us. We stir and wrestle and strain to see something different, something deeper. We have looked in all sorts of lesser places, shadow places that do not compare to the true light. We have tuned into frequencies that are muffled and garbled; we have settled for them and called them clear. But now the haunting leaves us uneasy and discomforted.

The more uneasy we are, the more we begin to see the breaks in the story, the shudders in the flattened fiction. We see how things are repeated and repackaged. The glitter fades away and the sleight of hand loses its luster, exposing the manipulation and distraction for what it is. The cognitive dissonance is too much. The more we pay attention, the more we notice that something *is* off, something is cheap and false about our existence in the cave.

The Ember

Let's be honest. The cave is intoxicating. Most of the time, we are comfortable in this system. The haunting Voice remains mildly intriguing but rarely compelling, because we feel safe in the familiar. The loneliness is awfully sad, but it's what we know. We've learned how to numb it enough to get by. Maybe we really are happy after all, aren't we? Isn't everything pretty good here in the cave? The risk of stepping out is too great, so we carry on within the cave, privately and secretly acknowledging the haunting Voice but never being brave enough to listen to it. We carry it, like a small ember or a flickering wick.

Once we've heard the Voice, it doesn't go away easily. It's radioactive.

We learn to hold onto that ember in private. We

might fan it a little bit, but ultimately, we keep it hidden. To do anything else threatens our safety and our comfort. If we are honest with ourselves, the ember threatens our own bliss, the one-dimensional part of ourselves that knows how to push the happy button and numb the pain away. We continue to access what is so readily available in the cave: the lesser loves, the lesser lights, the lesser lives.

We often can't articulate this, but when we hear the story of the cave we shrug and admit, "Yeah, that's life." Only *it isn't life*. It is a meager, broken existence.

What if it's true that we were meant to experience life to the full?

If we can come to the place where we realize that this ember is real, we begin to awaken. We realize that we are willing to risk it all. We realize we are ready to die to the comforts and conveniences of the cave, all for the possibility that this Voice is leading us somewhere true. The tension becomes too great in our spirits, and we cannot ignore the ember any longer.

In C.S. Lewis' classic, *The Silver Chair*, two human children and a very interesting character named Puddleglum find themselves trapped in Underland, a world below the real world. Underland is a deep, dark, cave-like world that exists below the surface, but doesn't acknowledge in any way that the whole land of Narnia flourishes above it. The longer the children and Puddleglum remain in Underland, the more they forget the Narnia they once knew. The evil queen of Underland bewitches them and tells them that they have only imagined the world above. They all but forget the truth of who they are and where they came from.

In the climax of the story, when the evil queen is about to have her vengeance and victory, Puddleglum finds his ember, deep within his consciousness where the Dark Magic couldn't snuff it out. He chooses truth that he doesn't understand but that he cannot reject:

> *"Suppose we have only dreamed, or made up, all those things - trees and grass and sun and moon and stars and Aslan himself. Suppose we have. Then all I can say is that, in that case, the made-up things seem a good deal more important than the real ones. Suppose this black pit of a kingdom of yours is the only world. Well, it strikes me as a pretty poor one. And that's a funny thing, when you come to think of it. We're just babies making up a game, if you're right. But four babies playing a game can make a play-world which licks your real world hollow. That's why I'm going to stand by the play-world. I'm on Aslan's side even if there isn't any Aslan to lead it. I'm going to live as like a Narnian as I can even if there isn't any Narnia."*[5]

Oh friend, the Voice of Truth tells you the story that you already know. Can you see the flames of the ember alive within you?

Giving up the false narrative sets us free. The ember begins to illuminate our very hands that hold it, and we see our created being, and it causes us to wonder. We then become aware of our arm, our torso, our whole body. We see our silhouette illuminated, and those of the people next to us. We see the darkness around us and it is stark and cold compared to the ember of a flame we now possess. The brightness tells the story of our creaturehood. We are meant for life and beauty, not death and decay in this cave. We see the beauty of our being, and then we realize: if we are a creature, then we came from somewhere.

The Wholly Other

If we are creatures, then we have a Creator. Curiosity compels us to awaken, listen, and search for the source of this life and beauty.

We know it's there. The haunting Voice has told us so, and perhaps we are finally brave enough to encounter Him. We are brave not because we understand His nature or because we trust Him just yet ... no, we are brave because somewhere in His haunting song, we heard Him sing of love.

Beloved.

Rudolph Otto introduces the concept of a "Wholly Other"[16] – a "Numen" as a "presence of divinity that unsettles us."[17] His use of the word "numinous" reminded him of the word "ominous", which elicits the sense of a dark, foreboding presence. The characters in another beloved C.S. Lewis masterpiece describe this well when they speak of Aslan the lion:

> *"Aslan is a lion- the Lion, the great Lion."*
>
> *"Ooh," said Susan. "I'd thought he was a man. Is he - quite safe? I shall feel rather nervous about meeting a lion…"*
>
> *"Safe?" said Mr. Beaver… "Who said anything about safe? 'Course he isn't safe. But he's good. He's the King, I tell you."*[18]

We glimpse the holiness and glory of this Wholly Other, this Perfect Love. Otto writes of an encounter with an all loving but all-powerful being who made him "shudder." The truth is not that we are made for another place; it is that we are made for another *person*. A Wholly Other. If we have seen Him, we have seen the Numen. We have seen the Creator and sustainer of all things. This awakening is where the creature and Creator relationship moves towards realignment.

So how do we find Him, then? This Numen, this Creator, this God of Love?

Broad to Specific

There is a path to encountering the heart of God in the person of Jesus. Before we can truly see Him and understand His perfect love for us, we are compelled on a journey that reveals it.

The broad view begins with creation itself. Most honest people can point to an experience in nature where they have felt the stirring of awe and reverence for the beauty around them. What is it about the vast mountains and the splendid daffodils, the sound of boisterous laughter and the unique raise of a person's eyebrow, the roar of the stormy wind and the silence of the starlit night that have inspired humanity throughout the ages? It's the mark of a Creator. The whisper on the wind is His song. The glory of creation points to the Creator. It reveals the Wholly Other. And if we slow down long enough to notice it, His presence begins to reveal itself to us.

As we narrow our gaze in the attempt to find the Wholly Other, our imaginations offer a conception of Him. Through the ages of humanity, we have fashioned a version of God based on the observable evidence around us. Many tribes and nations throughout the centuries have established belief systems and practices that acknowledge the awakening of a Presence. World religions have been birthed out of our attempts to name and define God, but most offer only a starting point to discovering the Wholly Other.

And yet, one Voice *keeps speaking* throughout the centuries: Israel's God. The God who simply says, "I AM".[19] The Word of this God was first spoken in creation, then carried in the voice of prophets, announced by angels, made flesh, and is now the living witness of the Spirit. This Spirit of Jesus is the Voice that we long for. It is the Voice of Perfect Love calling us to Himself.

Like being called from the outer perimeter of a field where the land spreads vast and open, we must travel across the field, coming closer and closer to the One who is speaking.

So many of us stop too soon.

As a young man, a group of my friends and I once tried to get into an abandoned house in the dead of night. The house was magnificent, like a castle or huge chalet that you might find in a storybook. The large windows were shuttered, the doors were regal, and the roofline had peaks and chimneys that added a dimension of magic. It seemed dangerous to even approach the property because of the stories we had heard of its owner, a notorious gun runner. Needless to say, we were scared. Something about it made me want to run away from it but that very something also made me want to run *toward* it.

We were so compelled to discover what was inside that we found ourselves on the grounds one night, peering through windows and trying doors until we finally found a way inside. There was something electrifying in the threshold moment, looking at the way in. Decades later, I can still feel it. We couldn't help but encounter the mysterious majesty of this house, and yet to enter it we had to find the way that had been left open. And when we did, a flood of anticipation pulsed through our veins.

The first steps inside were a terrifying victory. We had no right to be there, and yet there we were. Our feet were touching what felt like sacred ground. There were chandeliers and a few pieces of furniture still in the house, and it was in perfectly haunted condition. My heart pounded loudly as I made my way up the stairs, I was certain the owner could hear me, whether or not he was there, in prison … or dead.

Every room was empty, with few traces that someone had lived there. There was nothing of the guns and treasure we imagined. But what I did find that day remains with me for a lifetime. I remember standing in an upstairs bedroom, looking outside to the wooded driveway through the window. All of the wonder and dread and adrenaline had mixed and settled by then, and what remained was deep a satisfaction and a strange joy.

I had found the way in.

If we had given up when we touched the exterior wall of the house, or when we found the first locked door, we would have never discovered what was inside. It would have been like following the haunting Voice of the Wholly Other to the threshold of the cave and then not risking the next step. We would have wished that we had looked a little further, pushed a little more, searched until we had found.

So many of us stop too soon.

Remember the story of Celidonius? The Voice in his story started like a broad echo, a whisper that stood out against the everyday noises. But this man born blind heard the Voice of Jesus, and recognized His authority, His uniqueness. He recognized Him as being Wholly Other. His encounter with this powerful yet peaceful Voice was his invitation to see, to leave the cave of shadows for life to the full. He walked out of the cave – following, listening, awake – but still blind. He walked *without sight*, following the Voice that called him until his feet bumped into something and the Voice stood right in front of him. The very breath of God brushed on Celidonius' face.

So, how do we find ourselves at the feet of the Creator, in the presence of the Wholly Other, in the arms of Perfect Love?

Awake and Free

More than anything, we long to know *who* is behind that Voice. We have felt shackled at the neck, but again we turn our head. This time we twist a little farther and realize that where we *thought* we were shackled, that power has been broken. Broken.

How can this be?

The Wholly Other Himself is in the cave. *God with us*: *Immanuel*. Immanuel sets captives free and gives sight to the blind; but not so that we can move about the cave or see better in the cave. *Immanuel sets us free*. He enters the cave, and in His humble and merciful way he reminds us who we are. He speaks truth and grace and breaks the chains that have held us for so long.

In a terrifying and defining moment, we realize that we are free to walk out of the cave, the flattened fiction, the one-dimensional bliss. Finally, we can follow the Voice we've heard for so long – the one we heard but ignored. The one we numbed and avoided. The one we mistrusted and ridiculed. The one we hated for poking at our loneliness. The one we longed for in the deepest places of our souls.

And so, we walk toward the light.

We catch our breath, perhaps for the first time, as we approach the threshold of the cave. We are conscious of the voices calling us back into the darkness of the cave, but now *they* sound more like the haunting lies, and the Wholly Other sounds like the Truth. We were never meant to be in the cave in the first place. Something deep within us now knows that not only have we discovered a cure for the aching loneliness of our souls, but we have also found the source of Life itself.

The massive search for the haunting Voice has

drawn us to this place. We are awake. We are aware. We are brave and vulnerable, terrified and yet hopeful.

We are ready to see.

Jesus, Perfect Love Himself, Immanuel meets us at the threshold of the cave and asks us the most important question in all of life: "Who do you say I am?"[20]

That is the Voice! We recognize it: He who is not safe but good. The Wholly Other, the Numen. The Voice belongs to Him, we are sure of it now. He has asked us a question, and it is our turn to give an answer.

"Who do you say I am?"

This is the beginning of life to the full. To ignore this question is to stay in the dark, shackled to death and darkness, lonely and angry and *oh so afraid*. To invite this question is to step boldly towards life and beauty and freedom.

Section Two

Vision Up

Sight

I look up, and for the first time, I see.
Shadow. Then light.
The great I Am.
Could it be?
Could His embrace be the beginning
Or perhaps end of my search?
He is not what I expected.
He is everything I have longed for.
I Am.
The Face of Perfect Love.
Now I see.

Confession

I have seen the Wholly Other.
Perfect Love took on flesh.
Truth wells up within me,
Overflowing in my mouth and my heart and my soul.
He is God, and I am not.
I am creature, and He is Creator.
More than Creator.
He is Father. He is Perfect. He is Love.
I am brought low. I am unsettled.
I am recalibrated, set right.
Chaos is ordered, and it is very good.
Now I see.

Adoration

Perfect Love.
The face of my Creator.
My affection is aimed at Love itself.
The desire to worship swells and then bursts,
Alleluia! Songs of praise, prayers, and joy.
I dance and laugh and eat and drink.
Old, dusty garments of fear and confusion fall off.
The mundane becomes holy,
Everything an instrument of praise.
All of life is worship,
Returning love to the source from which it came.
Now I see.

Sight

VISION UP
LOOK TO HIM

Confession

Adoration

VISION IN
LOOK LIKE HIM

VISION OUT
LOOK WITH HIM

VU

O

VI

CHAPTER FOUR

Sight

We should be astonished at the goodness of God,
stunned that He should bother to call us by name,
our mouths wide open at His love,
bewildered that at this very moment
we are standing on holy ground.

Brennan Manning

Sight: the first vantage point on the trail of Life to the Full. We look to Him, and then we look like Him, and then we look with Him, over and over and over again. Every shift in the heart leads us to the next. The time has come to truly see, for the first time, who has been calling to us.

Consider for a moment what the haunting Voice has been saying all along. *Beloved.* The heavens declare it, creation pours out this testimony day after day with majesty, beauty, and balance. Prophets and poets have whispered these words for generations reflecting the image of the God who speaks.

We stand right where Celidonius did: blind, but face to face with Jesus. Celidonius speaks like so many of us. "Who is he, sir? I want to believe in him." I imagine Celidonius' hands placed on Jesus' face, feeling for familiarity.

Jesus' answer is stunning. "You have seen him, and he is speaking to you." Our eyes are opened. Tears and relief and confusion and incredulity flood over us. We are face to face with the Truth. We look up at Him, our Father, our living and breathing God.

The *Voice* of God becomes *flesh*.

The vision is Jesus.

The Eternal Flame

As a child, I never had much interest in Sunday school or catechism class. I thought I had the whole salvation thing worked out. I preferred to spend my time at church chasing after childhood crushes and hiding in the pews.

Catechism class was a bit of a walk. From my little parochial school room I would round the gym, pass by the big doors at the end of the hallway, go up some stairs to cross the choir loft and then back down some stairs into the fireside room. I knew just how to plan my trek to obtain maximum girl-chasing and pew-hiding time. I waited in the right places at the right times and then drifted back, hid, got a drink of water, forgot something – you name it. This allowed me to conveniently separate from the pack and linger alone until they finally came looking for me.

From my vantage point in those days, believing in Jesus was a get-out-of-hell-free pass. It kept me from going to the place of fire and brimstone someday. And if I wasn't going to hell, I knew the flip side of that coin meant that I was going to heaven. Conversations about life, death, and Jesus usually revolved around *place,* not *person.* God Himself was never understood as the destination. All I knew was this: "If you're good and believe in Jesus, you go to heaven. If you're bad and don't believe the salvation prayer, you go to hell." The Creator of the creature, the actual person, was not talked about. *He* was not the vision. Heaven was. I had never glimpsed or spent time with the idea of God and therefore had never thought about knowing God, or seeing Him in the flesh of His son. Somehow, I missed all of that.

I missed Jesus.

And yet ... He never stopped calling to me.

Many times, when I was trying to avoid class, I would find myself alone, lingering in the sanctuary, or hiding in a pew, avoiding the teaching about this religion that I had no interest in. And while I thought I was escaping God in those moments, even then I was drawn to something mysterious that compelled me to *look up*.

The sanctuary had an eternal flame that hung

from the ceiling at the front– a single, red vase with a solitary candle, always burning. It captivated me. The soft, muted, constant light enchanted me. I often looked at it for so long that my vision was red. Even when my mind was disengaged, fully yet unconsciously enmeshed into the narrative of the cave, my vision was compelled upwards. Long before I knew that such a thing truly existed, I heard the whisper of Love.

I didn't know Jesus was the One I was looking for, until the day I finally saw Him.

Confounded by Jesus

"Who do you say I am?"

The Voice of the Wholly Other rings out with the most important question in all of life.

When we look up, and our blurry eyes clear, we behold exactly what it is we came out of the cave to see. Face to face with Jesus, we are met with something unexpected. We are *unpleasantly* surprised. Our mind, which struggles to abandon our old narrative, our old created order, yells, "Foolishness!"

We've heard the beautiful, echoing Voice that spoke of something more. We've awakened to the possibility of a life that, God help us, could be fuller than the one-dimensional, illusive bliss we've been surviving. These whispers of new life have been our longing and our restlessness. We came all the way through the journey of hearing His Voice, awakening, and looking up to see Him. Now we stand face-to-face with Jesus, our eyes wide open, and he asks us the question, "Do you believe? My child, do you believe? Do you want to see the Messiah?" Life to the full rests on our answer to this question. Heaven inhales and waits.

And we say, "No way!"

We take one look at Jesus, and we scoff and shake our heads. No way! The story has to be bigger than this! There's no way that all of the infinite, all of the Perfect Love, all of the good and the power and the mystery are contained in *this person*. How foolish this story is if it comes down to just one man, a baby for heaven's sake, a refugee child from a humble town gallivanting across the hillsides with a handful of followers.

It just doesn't make sense. All of our searching led us to an encounter with *this* man, a man who has no money or earthly riches, no beauty or majesty to attract us to him, held in low esteem with nothing special in his appearance. A man despised and rejected, a man familiar with suffering and pain,[21] marginalized, scandalized, pushed to the outer fringes of every community until he was made a spectacle of, mocked, spit on, and crucified on a cross. *This Jesus?*

It confounds the wisdom of the world that the Voice we have been hearing belongs to this One.

Here, we are stuck.

We came out of the cave for *this*?

We begin to hear the whisper of something else, something foreign and at the same time familiar. Just as we heard the Voice of the Wholly Other in the cave, beckoning us out into freedom, we start to hear the counter-whisper of the cave, calling us back to the safety of the darkness. It mocks us for our faith and taunts us for our courage. The sickly-sweet sound of its alluring voice confuses us, and something within us wants to run back to the comfort, wealth, status, power, pleasure, and other false wonders of the cave.

In the space between hearing and seeing, we made up our own image of God. We repeated it so often to ourselves that we almost believe this false image, even when face to face with the Truth. If we follow the Voice to the threshold of the cave, we get more and more interested in whom we might see and what our God might be like. But, much like the disciples of Jesus Himself, our self-manufactured expectations create enormous and painful disbelief when we finally see Him.

We stare at Him. Our minds are temporarily confounded, and yet our hearts are oddly drawn to this ordinary and unexpected person of Jesus.

The mouth of the cave yawns wide at our backs, beckoning us to retreat to the familiar instead of engaging what we do not understand. We must look a little longer here, truly look at Him. As we do, we resist the counter-whisper of the cave that promises comfort but brings only bondage. There is Someone here that is worth knowing, Someone who calls us beloved. Jesus called us and calls us still, with a Voice that speaks to a deeper place within our soul than the cave voice ever could.

Perfect Love

This Jesus is nothing like we expected ... but He is everything we've ever hoped for.

Can it be true? Are we looking upon the face of Perfect Love? Have we truly found the One who can release our pain and sickness and fear and loneliness and brokenness?

"Who do you say I am?" He asks again.

There is little else in all of life that can compare with this experience of encountering Jesus. A new chamber opens in our hearts, birthing capacity to love and experience love that was not present before. The closest comparison I can think of to this encounter with Perfect Love was the day I became a father for the first time.

Bella was born just after 1 a.m. on January 9th of 2007. She came early, weighing only 4 pounds and 1 ounce. I was 29 years old at the time. I had spoken of love in sermons, been invited to share of love in speeches, and written about love in songs. I thought I had experienced love as deeply as it could be experienced. But early that morning, as I sat with Bella in the NICU, it was like the river of my love plunged over a waterfall, pouring into a vast sea that I could have never imagined in my wildest dreams. My hand was resting on her body, hidden almost completely in her blanket. I couldn't hold back my tears. The usual places in my mind that I go to quell my emotions weren't even touching the source of these feelings. A new love was drawing the tears from a place much deeper within me.

How could something so small punch through the deep, core layers of my heart and unlock a new reservoir of love? What power was it that she held? I thought I had loved her before she was born, but I now realized I had only loved the idea of her. Seeing her in the flesh, meeting her in person, kindled a love within me that went beyond anything I had ever experienced. Bella, hours old and in so many ways powerless, made visible the most powerful force that we can know. In her I came to understand the love of a father. Her life welcomed me into something that I had never known or encountered before. Looking at her, holding her, hearing her breathing... these are the things that plunged me into the vastness of love.

Twelve years later, each of my children have this effect on me. Being a dad unlocks parts of my heart and teaches me the ever-expanding nature of love. Seeing

Bella on the day she was born awakened me to a life-long journey that I would get to experience with her, the journey of my love for her coming fully alive. This is true with all of my children; love is always and ever expanding.

This is something of what happens when we meet Jesus. When we truly see Him, we discover the gateway to the infinite. He unlocks something deep within us and welcomes us into a relationship where we can experience and know and flourish in a Truth that has been there since the beginning.

You made me. You formed me. You see me. You have seen every broken part of my life and my heart, and yet you pursue me. You know me. You love me. What grace, what fidelity, what power and yet what holiness. You sacrifice yourself that I may become holy too. What mystery. What perfection. WHAT LOVE.

The One who created us and calls to us also comes to us. He entered the cave to set us free. He so loves His creation that *He poured out His life so that ours might be full.* This is the story of Israel's God. The God of Abraham, Isaac, and Jacob. The Creator, the Numen, the Wholly Other.

We hear His question again, "Who do you say I Am?"

In the grand and glorious moment of looking up, we find ourselves brought low. We find ourselves finally ready to give an answer to His question. We find ourselves ready to declare the truth of who He is and of who we are. When we truly see Him, we can do nothing else but desire Him more than all that we have or all that we know.

We are overcome. We fall to our knees, weeping in the magnificence of the Truth that is before us. The answer to His question opens the door to life like we have never known before: life to the full.

You are Jesus! The One I have been searching and longing for. The One I was made by and for. The Voice in the darkness, the whisper on the wind.

And here is where the story gets even better. We see the selflessness of His love, and we know that we are forgiven. We are forgiven for the mistakes we made in the cave. We are forgiven for allowing ourselves to become our own gods. We are forgiven for the ways we have grieved the Creator. We understand, as we look to Him, that His desire is not to punish us for these things. *His desire is to set us free.*

In this moment we realize we are not only seeing Jesus … we are seeing the Father. The Creator. God in His Perfect Love compels us into communion with Himself in the person of Jesus. Everything we believed about life and beauty in the cave falls away, because we find a new conception of life and beauty altogether. We have a new point of reference, a new framework of reality, a new understanding of all creation.

The vision is Jesus.

Now I See.

CHAPTER FIVE

Confession

Go now and then for fresh life.
Go whether or not you have faith.
Go up and away for life; be fleet!
I know some will heed the warning.
Most will not, so full of pagan slavery is
the boasted freedom of the town,
and those who need rest and clean snow and sky the most
will be the last to move.

John Muir

We see Him. We see the Perfect Love that we have been longing for. If we looked back in the distance, we could still see the entrance to the cave. But we look *up* and see *Jesus*. He is now our vision. We begin to grasp who and what it is that we were looking for, and it drops us low, face in the dirt, unsettled and breathless in wonder and awe that the true thing is true.

We know it is True– because we see Him.

There is a pressure here, a weight. Or perhaps it is more of a gravity, one that pulls us down to the dust of the earth, reforming and recalibrating us in our experience of life outside of the cave, life as it was designed to be lived. In the moment that we are brought low in the presence of the holy, we simultaneously experience a lifting of the weight of the world. It no longer rests upon us, for we are not our own gods.

He is God.

He is God, and we are not.

Our past is forgiven, cleansed, redeemed.

Our present is provided for, witnessed, upheld.

Our future is known by the One who is love. We are His. He is ours. We are safe, accepted, and cherished. We are no longer at the center, and we are not alone.

For the first time, and then for all time, we can release the truest and most liberating confession: *You are God, and I am not.*

Here we enter a new space, a formative space, where we experience the beginning of the disintegration of our idolatry and false visions of ourselves and the world, while at the same time receiving the overwhelming grace and favor of the Father. There is a pause here, and a very special place of rest. Before we can respond in worship, we must *receive*. We wait, then, allowing our hearts and minds to experience the wonder of life in union with the Wholly Other.

Creature and Creator

Creaturehood is an inconvenient truth. In the cave, we mask this identity more and more with machines that conceal the vulnerabilities of the flesh. While true peace eludes our souls, we find physical and psychological safety in new "armor" that is fashioned for a world *we* are creating. These are the new coverings in which we hide to conceal even the memory that we are created.

Before we fully receive the love our Creator is longing to give us, this armor must fall. We must return to a world we *actually* inhabit, but did not create. We confess that we are creatures, unmasking the pride of our age. To look *to* Him is to return as creatures to His presence. This is what Jesus spoke of when He said that He came to give life to the full.[22]

Colossians tells us that we were made by Him and for Him.[23] God himself created us for Himself. There's a relationship that is set up with us as creature and Him as Creator. The whole story, the whole of our DNA, all of our desire and longing is for that source to be embraced. Until we, the creatures, find ourselves face to face with the Creator, we will be restless. Distractions will multiply, and *nothing will satisfy*.

But when we, the trembling, mysteriously

curious creatures, find the way to this new place, we get a glimpse of something different. Not a glimpse of words on paper, or flannel pieces on a wall at Sunday school class, or a degree behind our name, or place on a pew in a cathedral. We glimpse the Creator himself. The reward is the relationship with the One who longs to be with us.

Being Humbled

There's a difference between *being humble* and *being humbled*. We can certainly hope to engage our lives from a posture of humility, but for that to flow freely, for us to choose to be humble, we must first *be humbled*. We are dropped low by the experience of an encounter with the Creator himself.

Mary Magdalene had this experience following Jesus' death and resurrection. She was the last to leave His tomb after He died and the first to return after the Sabbath. When she came back and found the tomb empty, she was distraught and confused. Then Jesus appeared to her. At first, she did not recognize Him, but when He called her by her name and revealed Himself to her, she found herself face to face with the Wholly Other. In that moment everything in her life changed.[24]

Similarly, when the disciples had been out fishing all night and came to shore without a catch, Jesus instructed them to cast their nets on the other side of the boat. Again, they did not recognize Him, but did as He suggested, and were overwhelmed with a net full of fish. Peter's eyes were opened, and he fell down and worshipped.[25] He was humbled, brought low in the presence of the Wholly Other. Moses came face to face with God near the burning bush,[26] and Joshua at Gigal.[27] These people shared a similar experience of coming face to face with the Wholly Other, the Numen, the Creator that opened their eyes, humbled them, and dropped them low.

We are humbled when we see Him, when we are face against the dirt, pressed upon the dust of the ground, in the presence of the holy.

Into the Wild

Our family cabin at Diamond Lake has a perfect view of Mt. Thielsen where it touches on the eastern edge of the water. In the morning, when the sun comes up, light dances on the water and shines through the pines. Diamond Lake is a shallow lake, lined with dead trees whose roots can't hold because they grow in dry, pumice soil. On each side of the lake, bone-dry jagged limbs reach out and grab at your clothing when you pass by.

I love this place. There can be snow in July, or warm days all the way into September. Our cabin has one room, no plumbing, and a cache of old comic books that feel new again each year we come to visit. The moment the front door opens, the smell of a wood stove, maple syrup, and Pendleton wool washes over us. It's perfect, every time.

As soon as my feet touch that ground, I become a child again. The silence shuts my mouth and the enormity of the trees open my eyes. It doesn't matter if it is the middle of an October night during hunting season or the late afternoon heat of a summer day; it's not the season, it's the place. I hear only the wind in the trees, the deep drawing in and pushing out of mountain air. No one moves, certainly not me.

> *No guru, no method, no teacher.*
> *Just you and I and nature*
> *And the Father in the garden.*[28]

That's how it feels. In the beauty and silence, my heart swells.

In the wild, we remember who we are: *creatures*. We need to remember that, more often than we think. It's good to be out in nature and admit that we live in a world we didn't create and cannot control. It's even better to be immersed in it, reminded that we were not here first. I am not a total anti-technology, granola, Wendell Berry loving Oregonian … but I am convinced that a little more John Muir and John Denver could do the world some good. A little more fresh air, a little more silence, a little more intentional witnessing of the glory that surrounds us.

Our creaturehood is becoming harder and

harder to see, a dangerous trend that will only continue to advance. Our culture, our education, and our experience all mask it. We create and control our environments: buildings, cities, technologies, our homes, and even our clothing. We increasingly disconnect from nature, finding ourselves encountering the external world mediated by screens or some integration of man and machine. It is no coincidence that most people say that they feel closest to God when they are outside – not in the backyard they just mowed, but out in a vast ocean or a grand forest or listening to the symphony of birds in a park or by a stream. *It is our natural habitat.*

We are creatures in captivity only insomuch as we choose to be.

Go into the wild and be small. Find it. Find your place. The tree in your yard or near your home is good, but *push farther*. Find the holy ground, the spot where beauty and silence shut your mouth and open your eyes. "Go up and away for life." Touch the earth again. Get outside and take a breath. Stay until you feel unsettled … and then wait. Be present there. When the five minutes of silence is about all you can take, wait longer. Feel and embrace the miraculous tension of being alive.

The counter whisper of the cave works hard to convince us that such a practice isn't necessary. Of course it does; such life and beauty will shatter any desire within us to ever return to the flattened fiction. We hear the counter whisper mocking our choice to embrace our creaturehood in the wild, haunting our efforts to truly see. We resist the cave voice by choosing to surround ourselves with the truth of creation.

Go outside. Please. Not on a one week a year vacation, but every day. Every single day - a ritual of remembrance. Take off your shoes and feel the ground. Release the weight of the world in exchange for the peace of the birds who do not worry. Work the ground, water something, plant a flower, feed a bird, and spare a spider. Touch some dirt or pick a weed or put your foot in a river or lay on a blanket and watch the sun dance between the leaves and between your toes and just breathe. Remember that you are not in the center of the created world, and that you are not alone.

In the wild, we remember that we are creatures. The confession wells up within us: He is God, and we are not. He is God, and we are not. *He is God, and we are not.* We are overcome, and we are loved.

Rest and Receive

We squat a lot in religion. We are neither standing nor kneeling, neither leveled nor lifted. We are in a wall sit, straining our muscles to hold the weight of our whole selves while also trying to acknowledge some greater deity. Religious squatting is *tiring*.

Yes, we are tired. Exhausted, really. We are longing to receive the life that we have ventured out of the cave to find. We are like travelers in need of a long, hot bath. We need to rest and receive even more than we think we do. It is in the moments we confess the truth, *He is God and we are not*, that we begin to receive. The squatting posture breaks, the wall-sit collapses, and as we rest upon the earth we are brought back to the origin of our identity.

An outcropping on the Oregon coast overlooks the expanse of the Pacific. From that spot, that last inch of land on the western coast, I sometimes watch the Creator color the sky and animate the wind and the waves. "For the life of every living thing is in his hand, and the breath of every human being."[29] Every time I sit there and watch the sun plunge into the sea, I learn it all over again. That's my prayer: that witnessing His created world would lead us again and again to a deeper relationship with Him.

> *The heavens proclaim the glory of God.*
> *The skies display his craftsmanship.*
> *Day after day they continue to speak,*
> *night after night they make him known.*
> *They speak without a sound or word;*
> *their voice is never heard.*
> *Yet their message has gone throughout the earth,*
> *and their words to all the world.*[30]

Nothing can give rest to our eyes and tune our ears to the Voice of the Creator like time in His studio. This is not a call to retreat from revelation but to be immersed in it. His beauty and our silence allow us to see. May it never be said of us that "those who need rest and clean snow and sky the most" were the last to move. Where will you go? Where is that place you long to discover or return to, to be unsettled, to feel small, and to remember who you are?

Recalibration

These are the essential elements of our confession: rest, receiving, and recalibration. As we wait and breathe, we experience the wonder and fragility and beauty of creaturehood. We feel like children again. Free. Loved. Secure. Something inside of us adjusts, not to demolish and reconstruct our framework for viewing the world, but to recalibrate it to what it was always designed to be.

The weight of the world lifts, because we no longer have to carry it. Again and again, each time we go into the wild, each time we choose to rest and receive, we are recalibrated to a true understanding of who we are and how He loves us. Rediscovering our creaturehood allows us to understand our identity - our *vulnerability, capacity and responsibility.*

The view of our *vulnerability* is recalibrated when we realize our smallness, our powerlessness. We don't like to think of ourselves this way, especially because our cave programming had us believing that we were gods in our own right. And yet, the truth remains. Our agency and potency ironically come from our proper understanding of this dissonant concept. So much is outside of our control. The armor we have put on will do nothing to truly protect us. In the stillness of the night, when we are alone, we comprehend that our hopes, fears, dreams, desires, plans, failures, and accomplishments are hardly even blips on the cosmic radar screen. It is good for us to feel this. It is good for us to feel dependent. It is good for us to feel our limits. This is what is real.

And yet, though it makes no sense to us, we know that we mean everything to our Creator. We understand that all the pieces of our individual lives matter, that they in fact *are* significant to the only One who loves us perfectly. We are small, weak, negligible … and yet at the same time so completely loved, valued, and desired. This recalibration allows us to see and receive the incredible and paradoxical truth about our vulnerability.

The view of our *capacity* is recalibrated when we realize that we are children of God. We are heirs, the beloved, the chosen. This is our capacity, our identity. This sets us free from fear, anxiety, and the false expectations that we created for ourselves when our faith was in the works of our own hands. This freedom allows us to rediscover that our real capacity is our ability to wonder and to think, to act, to feel, and to create along with the Creator, other creatures, and creation itself.

The view of our *responsibility* is recalibrated when we discover our true purpose, our true reason for living: to love Him back. Life from this point on becomes a great adventure of discovery as we pursue the question: *what does it look like for me to love Him back?* We each find unique ways of answering this question – some find it in community, some in liturgy, some in creativity. Some find it in music or poetry or paint. Some find ways to serve the creation itself, the earth; some find ways to serve their fellow creatures with reflections of the love they have received from the Creator. Some find ways unique only to themselves. Whatever our individual answers are to the question, our collective response to this recalibration all comes down to one thing: adoration.

CHAPTER SIX

Adoration

Holy, Holy, Holy
Lord God Almighty,
All Thy works shall praise Thy name
In earth and sky and sea!

Reginald Heber

We see. We confess. We love our Creator back. Though we are brought low by the weight of His glory, we are simultaneously lifted up by the beauty of His love. Our souls breathe, and we exhale in a posture of awe and reverence. We no longer look at circumstance, hoping it will lock eyes with us and grant us our desire. We look at and lock eyes with Perfect Love. Finally, there is peace. This is the next vantage point on our trail: adoration.

Adoration is the opposite of the expressions of love in the cave. Cave love is a love directed only at ourselves. It's shaped by the belief that we are alone in the center, fearing others and competing for scarce resources.

Adoration, on the other hand, is the overflow that comes when we truly realize that we are not alone, that we are valued and cherished, and that Perfect Love provides for our needs.

In our pursuit of life to the full, adoration may be the most important word to understand because it takes us to the source. In practice, adoration is giving expression to our highest affections. But how do we return love to Perfect Love? What is Love's love language? We have to find out what pleases the Lord in order to love Him back. This means knowing Him. We can begin with the scriptures, which speak of justice, mercy, compassion, gentleness, beauty, self-control, kindness, grace, and many other ways of returning love back to the source.

First Position

We are creatures created to adore our Creator. Adoration is woven into our DNA. It is our "first position": the original posture of the creature before the Creator. This posture is the place from which all human flourishing flows. No wonder we emerge from the cave gaunt, soul-starved, and gasping. We are like dislocated bones trying to walk. We have spent our lives in the cave *out* of first position. Now, we intentionally enter a space that we tried so hard to avoid in the cave. First position is the return of the head, heart, and hands to the source – our fully integrated being now animating in relationship. This is pleasing to God but essential to us, because this connection re-enchants life itself.

With the creature/Creator relationship restored, all of life, all of our expressions, whatever we eat and drink and whatever we do, the fullness and animation of our life becomes the expression of our affection.[31] Everything becomes holy - the cooking, the washing up, the hard conversations, the visits to the doctor, the laundry, the hours of office work, the conversation with the person in the check-out line. In the hands of a creature that loves God, *everything* becomes a way of returning love to the source. We learn to remain in this "first position" of adoration as we engage the world we live in. We long to remain in this first position because it is the place where the love within us can return to its source.

When we think back to Celidonius, we recall that he came face to face with the Wholly Other. The darkness that had enveloped his life since birth was lifted and he found himself in the presence of light. For the first time, he saw the radiance of physical light and the glory of God. In that strange and beautiful moment his new heart experienced the fullness of receiving *and* returning the love of God.

Adoration is the response of a new heart. It is love responding to love and therefore it returns only what it has received. Maybe Paul had this in mind when he wrote his letter to the church in Rome reminding them to offer their bodies as "living and holy sacrifice".[32] He told them to keep God's love in full view so that their love would flow from the source. We can return or give only from what we have received. I say that again. We can return or give only from what we have received. This return happens in the first position of adoration.

It's Only True if It's True

Without vision of God Himself, without being unsettled and brought low by His love, loving Him back becomes mechanical and mathematical. It's like knowing that the Pacific touches the edge of the west coast but never being close enough to be moved by the crash of its waves. Never swimming in it. Never being carried by its surf, or dazzled by the dying sunlight that dances on its waters at dusk. And here's the thing: never experiencing the Pacific doesn't make it any less magnificent. But it does mean that we miss something beautiful and powerful. Life without adoration does not diminish the glory of God; it diminishes *us*. It diminishes our experience of and participation in His glory.

Adoration brings life... but *it's only true if it's true*. It does not and cannot exist in abstraction.

I have experienced the pain of a true thing not actually feeling true. I understood adoration at a head level, but I was deficient in the formation of my heart. I didn't have a vision for a life of adoration, so I struggled to walk it out in any real way. Adoration remained an abstraction, forced and awkward. I could say that I loved God, but only like a husband that says he loves his wife without being with her: never seeing her, hearing her, or showing her his love. I knew that I loved God, but didn't know how to actually see, hear, act, or express my affection for Him.

In actuality, it felt safer to love Him from a distance, because to be honest, I had another problem. I had no issue keeping God's love in view or trying to accept that He actually loved broken people. My problem was that I couldn't accept myself as one of those loved and broken people. I had unclean lips and guilty hands, a troubled mind and a wandering heart. For the longest time I didn't know what to do with those parts. My brokenness and not knowing how to love Him back allowed me to learn, but only because it brought me back to the dirt. I didn't know where else to go. I just knew that's where I belonged, and that if I was going to experience life to the full it would begin right there. So, I got low and waited, creature before Creator. And not just once or twice. I had no idea what to say or do, or if I should even say or do anything at all. I just kept going back and waiting. Most of the time the only thing I could say honestly was, *I don't know what to do, but my eyes are on you.*[33]

In the strange beauty of the dust, life to the full begins. In the beginning, I was awkward in His presence, learning that I was His and He was mine, that I had not only been made by and for Him, but that He loved me as His creation and I loved him as my Creator. But over time that awkwardness gave way to rest, and in resting I learned to adore Him. Like the prodigal son, I had returned to something far more than a place. I had returned home. My guilty hands were washed. My heart was made new and my mind made whole. It was only then that my lips were unsealed.

That's how I learned to love him back. By being there and being honest. Simply bringing what I had, but no longer in abstraction. No faking. And it took time. The scriptures say that if we come close to Him he will come close to us.[34] They say, "What you say flows from what is in your heart."[35] Maybe the same is true about our physical bodies. My heart knew it was good to be near the Lord, but in order to be present there I had to change my posture. Looking back, I realize that the whole process was my recalibration. Each time I got low, and each time I humbled myself as creature before the Creator, physical body and all, my loves were being reordered. And little by little, the ceiling that had flattened my soul was giving way and crumbling and little shafts of light danced in my life.

The true thing became true.

From this true place, action emerges. Songs, acts of mercy, forgiveness, creativity, hospitality, serving others, preferring others, caring for the earth, laughing, and tasting the goodness of God. We can *know* what's pleasing to the Lord, but if we don't *act* on it, that love remains locked up within us - never reaching its aim, holding beauty captive.

This takes real effort. Saying, "I love you" can only become natural by saying, "I love you!" over and over again, in word and in mercy, justice, truth, and grace. These are not just pretty words. They are the realities of life to the full, the truth that becomes true as our loves are rightly ordered *and* expressed. Unfortunately, for many years in the church, I have walked alongside many men and women from many different backgrounds who love God deeply but have never experienced this. Their lives are the *opposite* of full. Their love for God remains captive, their religious expressions fine-tuned and calculated, yet they remain without joy and without communion.

Religious instruction can teach us to pray piously, sing beautifully, and serve faithfully, but if these acts are not done as expressions of love in communion with the Creator, they fall flat. We were made for more than dipping buckets in the water and throwing it over the side of the dam. Religious instruction should lead us to the source of the water. If we unleash love at the source, the power will break the dam simply because love is *that* powerful in and of itself. It breaks the dam doors wide open and every channel of our life is free to release love back to its source. Adoration will lead to action.

When we experience the feeling of "getting it but not having it", it is often because we move too quickly. We do not allow the realities of God to transform and renew our minds. We *speak* our adoration but don't act on it. We don't allow our fully integrated beings to be present in our worship, without distraction. But it doesn't have to be this way. We can begin to comprehend all of His majesty by slowing down and taking in what we see in creation. We see Perfect Love and experience the wonder of loving Him back.

A Habit of Devotion

This doesn't happen overnight. Of course, in our Instagram-fueled world we have been taught to believe that such things are possible. We can put a filter on almost anything and instantly call it very good. But in reality, there is no filter that instantly transforms or expands our ability to express love to God. Loving Him back to a place of flourishing takes time and careful attention. Rhythms and postures allow us to return love to the source. There must be sacred space and sacred time to pursue Him and engage Him. It requires intention to experience communion with the transcendent when our brains and bodies actually can't transcend space or time. Loving God back takes engagement and requires our whole being: heart, mind, soul, and strength. The goal is continual presence, where all of life becomes a loving return to the source.

Every created being is a unique instrument because of unique circumstance. There are expressions of love that can only be displayed in and through specific and individual lives. Think about that. In all of creation there is a song, a word, an act of grace or mercy or hospitality that can only be expressed through *you*. These are our signature expressions of love.

Imagine waking up in the morning and recalibrating your orientation to operate as you were intended to – from the first position of adoration. You look up and choose to love Him back. *Today, I will live my life as an expression of love back to the source. Today, my parenting will be a channel for love to flow back to God. Today, my vocation will be a channel for love to flow back to God. Today, I will look at myself in the same, loving way that God looks at me. Today, I will look to Him and every sphere of my life will open wide.* Imagine acting from that place. Imagine the life and beauty, the cleansing joy that would become visible in our lives.

Flourishing is Relational, Not Circumstantial

Years ago, I got a call from a good friend named Bryan. His voice was shaky, but he spoke clearly. "Zach, Liz's dad just died. He had a heart attack and is being transported to Newberg Hospital. I'm on my way, but you may get there before I do."

I looked at the clock, got up and began to make my way to the hospital. Though I was moving as quickly as possible, it felt like slow motion. I was wading through a deep feeling that time was moving, but I wasn't.

I was doing my best to stay ahead of the mental fog, but I could feel it settling in. On the drive, a million thoughts passed through my mind. I tried to imagine how things might go once I arrived. What to say. What not to say. What to do. Then I arrived. The hospital doors hesitated in front of me, staying shut just long enough for me to realize that none of that mattered. Once they opened, my friend was in my arms. All I could do was silently pray, "Lord, I don't know what to do, but my eyes are on you."

When we don't know where else to turn, we look up. When our wisdom, strength, and ability are completely stripped away, when looking around us or within us has produced nothing but heartache and frustration, we look up. When nothing in this world can provide the answers we are searching for, we look to a source, whether we even believe in one or not. It may be in anger, or in confusion, or in doubt, or in hope ... but eventually, we look up. In our weakest, most painful moments, our created nature will reach instinctively to the Creator.

My earliest recollection of this "reaching" came the day that my parents told me that my grandfather, "Grandpa Bob", had died. I don't even remember how old I was, but I remember running outside around the back side of my grandparents' house and collapsing in the dust. I remember crying and crying: no words, just pain. I remember the nagging question, *why?* Something deep within me knew to look up, even if, in a way, it was to point a finger. I had to. It was where I instinctively knew my help would come from. I was just a kid facing something huge – something terribly bigger than myself. E.M. Bounds describes prayer as "the outstretched arms of the child for the Father's help."[36]

I found this same soul posture when my wife and I lost our Aurora May to a miscarriage; I walked out on my back deck and looked up again. Even to this day, I realize that when all my strength is depleted, that is who I am. I am just a kid looking to my Father for help, and in my reaching I find Someone beautiful. It is in the deepest valleys that rivers of adoration flow. In these broken and helpless places, we can allow ourselves to be drawn deeper into the relationship that will sustain us and allow us to flourish.

At times we may travel deep valleys of tragedy, but often it is the long, slow walk in the desert of daily life that truly depletes our strength. The darkness experienced in our day to day struggles can be more suffocating than even the most piercing darkness that comes with sudden heartbreak. Often, I sit underneath the stars wrestling with a difficult decision. When I am in doubt and fear, frustrated with myself as a husband or dad, I will *look up*. Same posture and same prayer. "Lord, I don't know what to do, but my eyes are on you."

Life to the full is not free from painful circumstances. Life to the full means choosing and releasing love *in and through the circumstance.*

Flourishing is relational, not circumstantial. Flourishing does not mean that our bills are paid, our home is tidy, our friends are popular, or our jobs are prestigious. Flourishing means that *despite* any circumstance that may arise, we thrive in a place of love and joy and hope. We thrive in this place because of our relationship with Jesus.

I Love You, Lord

Every night, as I lay my son down to sleep, we sing this simple song.

> *I love you, Lord*
> *And I lift my voice*
> *To worship You*

Oh, my soul, rejoice!
Take joy my King
In what You hear
Let it be a sweet, sweet sound
In Your ear.[37]

This is the song of the new creation, the beat of new hearts, expressed in millions of forms through millions of creatures. I love you, Lord.

Vision Up, looking *to Him*, fosters a life of adoration. Adoration expressed transforms our daily life and re-enchants us to new perspectives. When we look up, we can't ever look down the same way again. With broken lips and broken lives, guilty hands and troubled minds, we begin to realize that we are created to say *I love you* to our Father. Our kind, merciful, and loving Father. It starts right there where the truth bubbles up.

It's relational, not circumstantial. When I wake up in the morning I wake up in relationship. Not in abstraction. Not alone. *I love you, Lord. I love you, Lord, and I lift my voice to worship You.* Say it louder! *I love you, Lord, and I lift my voice!* Water busts through a fissure from the source. *I love you, Lord, and I lift my voice to worship You! Oh, my soul, rejoice! Take joy, My King! My King!* Now our voices swell and we stomp and jump; the water rushes and floods our cracked lives and we sing and dance. *I adore you, Jesus!*

We are free.

I had a heart of stone, but God took that heart of stone and put a new heart in me. The chambers open up and everything pours back to Him. The songs I sing, the breakfast I make, the floor I sweep, the conversation I have, my response to the angry driver, and my reaction to being wronged all become worship. This truth colors every dimension of my life, infusing my thoughts, emotions, and actions with meaning.

The downstream effect of loving God back is life and beauty. Living a life of adoration is returning love to its source, with every minute, with every breath, with every activity under heaven. Not only the meditations of the mind or affection of the heart, but the work of our hands. Everything made holy. Everything shared in communion – creature and Creator. All of life a chorus soaring through creation, observed in the heavenly realms. A continual anthem – *we love you, Lord*. It rises in the morning and retreats quietly until there is no more night. We live in adoration.

Adoration is the *response,* not the source. Before I get out of my bed in the morning, I choose for my first conversation to be with God. With my eyes up, I orient to reality. Relationship. I'm still alive. I'm here. I'm grateful. I love Him. In this posture, I rise and start my day, ready to look more like Him.

Section Three

Vision In

Surrender

There is more.
The Wholly Other will not love from afar,
Nor am I content to let Him.
His desire is to be for me, and with me, and in me.
My life is to be a home for His
Perfect Love.
Light knocked on my door,
But I have no room for light.
How can this be?
The darkness must die.
A surrender. A death. A new life.
May it be.
Now I see.

Nurture

Perfect Love resides in me.
I am responsible to a life that I am not responsible for.
I am expectant.
I choose to nurture this gift above all else.
I seek only the good, only the true, only the beautiful.
I guard this life, careful now to do no harm.
Sacrifice is made for the sake of Another.
Love matures within.
Long, slow, deep.
I choose to love this life in me.
Now I see.

Transformation

I am ready.
I long to look just like my Father.
Young love lives in me,
Headstrong, adolescent, selfish, fearful.
I am yet marked by scarcity,
Needy and dependent.
His love is different.
Perfect.
Selfless, generous, and free.
Marked by abundance.
In the fullness of time,
Young love matures.
Redemption.
The image of Love restored in me.
Now I see.

CHAPTER SEVEN

Surrender

My soul's house is narrow for you to enter;
will you not make it broader?
It is in a state of collapse;
will you not rebuild it?
It contains things which must offend your eyes;
this I know and I admit.
But who will make it clean?
To whom, except you, shall I cry?

Augustine

We have reached a new point along our trail, a point where our gaze shifts. In the last section we looked up to behold our Creator, confessed the creaturehood of our true identity, and returned love to the source through adoration. Each essential part of the path leads us to the next. Having seen Jesus face to face, we now look *in* and begin to see His image in us.

There was a long period in my life where I had no desire to look like Christ. Why would I? I hadn't truly seen Him, and I certainly didn't *know* Him. My vision of God in those days was a Frankenstein mosaic that I had pieced together along the way. It was a narrative that, to be honest, I rather liked. It was a safe and definable story to live by. I could answer questions about Him, describe His attributes, and spout plenty of Bible trivia, but at the end of the day I didn't know Him. He was not my vision. He didn't unsettle me because He remained in my control. Smaller than me. A god of my making. Like a museum curator, I showed people the framed and sterile images of God, then closed up the museum and headed out to my *real life*.

We can exist like that for a time. I did. Alive but not full. Fine but not flourishing. This worked for me until I began to seriously consider asking Cammie to marry me. I was sitting on a porch one night in L.A., contemplating the future. I realized then and there that I wanted to marry her ... but I didn't want her to marry *me*. Not this guy. Not this mess. I knew I couldn't give her the love she deserved. My loves had distorted me. My past had broken me. My weaknesses defined me.

As I sat there, I felt a strong desire to become something different. I wanted her to experience real love. Mature love. I knew that *I* wasn't it, and yet I loved her enough to desire more for her. I wanted for it to come through me, but how? I was ready to surrender the "house of my soul", as Augustine puts it, so that it might be filled with love worthy of her.

The next day before hopping on a boat to propose, I stopped by a church. I sat in the back and listened to a sermon on Hosea, about breaking up the unplowed ground. As I listened that day, I began to hear the haunting Voice again, and this time it triggered a battle of pride and desire within me. My pride resisted surrender and yet my desire demanded it. The pastor gave an invitation for anyone who felt that they wanted God to break through the hardness of their heart to raise a hand so they could be prayed for. Three times he called, three times others in the room responded, and three times I resisted, rolled my eyes, and ignored the piercing conviction in my soul. And yet the haunting Voice kept speaking.

As he was closing the invitation, he said there was one person in the room still fighting surrender. I knew it was me. The word *surrender* burned like a brand on my heart. I took a breath, closed my eyes, and stood up. He prayed. I opened my eyes. In a room full of hundreds of people, I was the only one standing. I was undone. My heart has never been the same. The guy that walked into the church that day didn't walk out. I was someone new.

The mature love that I wanted for Cammie

didn't come immediately. I had to walk through the process of looking up first. I had to experience the process of seeing, the act of confessing, the rhythms of adoring. But as I walked the trail, my vision turned in, not with a spotlight *on* me but a searchlight *in* me. The house of my soul needed to be surrendered to the One who created it to be His house in the first place.

The Order of Things

Before we get too far into Vision In, we must remember this: looking in without first looking up is a dark and dangerous road. Rather than applaud those as brave who do it this way, we should admire those who wisely recognize that we are image bearers of Christ. The *whole* truth about us is found by first looking up, and *then* in. Looking in without first seeing and knowing our Creator is a painful trap that ensnares us in a loop of self-absorption. Two things can happen here. We either get stuck in Vision In or we skip Vision In completely because we haven't first looked up.

We've seen both extremes happen in ourselves, and in others, haven't we? Perhaps we've known someone who has spent years working on self-discovery, self-improvement, and inner spirituality. Perhaps, this resonates with you. After all of the inner looking, however, peace and joy remain elusive. Why? Because we skipped Vision Up. We bypassed the reality of God. Any sort of transformation from this place is egocentric and can't bring true flourishing because it remains committed to the cave-gods, the gods of our own making, or our own self-as-god.

Or the other extreme: skipping Vision In altogether. This idea seems noble, altruistic, and selfless. It looks loving. However, it becomes problematic when we go directly from Vision Up, looking to Him, to Vision Out, looking with Him. We will discuss Vision Out more fully in the last section. But, here's my point. When we look upon the created world with the intent to participate in its restoration *without* first looking like Jesus, we will see the world without mature love. We pour our love outwardly and yet we become frustrated, exhausted, and often resentful. When we skip Vision In, we cannot reflect His image, nor can we see as He does. We may have the best of intentions, but without Vision Up and Vision In we see the world in a distorted way.

But, we *should* participate in mending and restoring and bringing peace! Right? Isn't that the point? Why bother taking time to look at our own selves when the fate of the world is at stake? We should work hard in our churches and our families, with our co-workers and our social platforms, aiming to make a difference *somehow*. But this work cannot bring fulfillment until we have allowed the restoration work to begin in our own souls. Only when we look like Him can we see the world with His eyes. When we look outwardly and work outwardly, striving to direct missions and visions and programs that aim to bring people to Jesus, *without* first looking like Him, we hurt people. We end up tired, burnt out, struggling with a weight that we were never meant to carry.

This is why the order matters.

Vision Up, Vision In, Vision Out.

Experiencing *this* sort of internal vision is the essence of transformation. There is no other outcome — we cannot stay the same. We transform into the thing we were created to be: image-bearers of the Creator Himself. We begin to *look like Him*.

A New Reality

There's a scene in the movie *Act of Valor* where a Navy Seal commander boards a yacht belonging to a wealthy cartel leader. The Seals board, seize, and secure the vessel so that the commander can have a private conversation with "Christo", the head of a cartel. In a poignant scene, these two powerful figures, seated directly across from one another at a table, lock eyes. The commander says, "Let me tell you how the world really works. This is no longer your boat. Since I walked through that door, you're no longer the same guy you used to be. You're just not."[38]

They continue to have a conversation, but the

conversation happens in the *context of a new reality*. Everything changed the moment the Seals overtook the boat. Power shifted, roles shifted, identity shifted, relationship shifted. Christo was not the same man he used to be.

We are not used to that kind of sovereignty, the kind of reality-transforming presence that Jesus brings when He dwells within us. Everything must change. We must be born again by allowing the life of Christ to be "born" in us, to dwell, to make His home in us. "Anyone who belongs to Christ has become a new person. The old life is gone; a new life has begun!"[39] His presence makes all things new. It can't be any other way. Light and darkness cannot coexist. When light enters, darkness is *transformed*. Love always has the final word.

Christo's crew could put up an American flag, change uniforms, train the crew, and even declare the boat to be a U.S. Navy vessel. But no matter how diligently they tried or how loudly they shouted, it wouldn't have been true. *It's only true if it's true.* And it becomes true when the one with the true authority boards the vessel and takes command. In that moment, everything changes. Physically the boat remains the same, but its orientation, purpose, and identity have all changed.

In some ways, looking more like Him would be easier if the presence of God entered our lives like a Seal commander. It would be simpler if He would just subdue all resistance upon entry and seize control, initiating the change to make us look like Him without action or choice on our part. I have wished plenty of times that it worked that way. But it doesn't. He doesn't force us, ever. He enters only by our surrendering invitation. He dwells in a strange and paradoxical way. He could secure and subdue us at any moment, and yet He comes as He originally did 2000 years ago: in the most humble and gentle manner.

May It Be

Transformation means a continual surrender to the miracle of new life. It is not something we try for… *it is something we die for*. Surrender begins when we say, "May it be".

The most clear and dramatic portrayal of this experience in scripture is when God chose to place His very life within Mary. He chose to partner with her in bringing about the promise that the Word would become flesh. When she said, "May it be", her life was changed biologically, psychologically, socially, and spiritually. She was given the incredible opportunity to cultivate the life within her of a Son who would be sovereign over her. The very image of God was being formed in her and at the same time was forming her, conforming her to His image.

In the sixth month of Elizabeth's pregnancy, God sent the angel Gabriel to Nazareth, a village in Galilee to a virgin named Mary. She was engaged to be married to a man named Joseph, a descendant of King David. Gabriel appeared to her and said, "Greetings, favored woman! The Lord is with you!"

Confused and disturbed, Mary tried to think what the angel could mean. "Don't be afraid, Mary," the angel told her, "for you have found favor with God! You will conceive and give birth to a son, and you will name him Jesus. He will be very great and will be called the Son of the Most High. The Lord God will give him the throne of his ancestor David. And he will reign over Israel forever; his Kingdom will never end!"

Mary asked the angel, "But how can this happen? I am a virgin."

The angel replied, "The Holy Spirit will come upon you, and the power of the Most High will overshadow you. So the baby to be born will be holy, and he will be called the Son of God. What's more, your relative Elizabeth has become pregnant in her old age! People used to say she was barren, but she has conceived a son and is now in her sixth month. For the word of God will never fail."

Mary responded, "I am the Lord's servant. May

everything you have said about me come true." And
then the angel left her.[40]

Whenever I read this account, I hear myself echoing Mary's question: *how can this happen?*

This incarnation of the Creator within the creature is the greatest mystery in all creation. How can it be that He would take on flesh and dwell among us? That He would lay down His life to redeem ours, all so that He might come and dwell in us? This movement of the Spirit upon Mary was only the beginning of God dwelling within His people; the endgame was that every single created human could experience the transformation of receiving God within themselves. We were created by Love and for Love, made to bear the image of Perfect Love. Love itself is to be formed within us, to animate our thinking, acting, and feeling.

How can this be?

Mary's story allows us to peer into the mystery of a human life becoming the dwelling place of the Wholly Other. In dramatic portrayal, we witness Vision Up becoming Vision In and we are reminded that transformation in Christ is a miracle. It is not just a wondrous thing, but it is truly the most significant miracle that could possibly be imagined. God within us. The Creator within the creation.

Imitation or Incarnation

In my younger years, I had to learn a completely new understanding of spiritual transformation. I was accustomed to *trying* more than dying, *imitation* more than transformation. I believed that forcing myself through a process of information collection and discipline mastery would lead me to resemble Christ. I believed that the strength of my moral muscle would eventually develop a depth of spiritual maturity within me. I believed that looking *like* Him was a matter of my imitation *of* Him.

But I discovered it was not. Seemingly impossible, yet stunningly simple, the truth is this: transformation in Christ is not about intellectual mastery, religious piety, or devoted disciplines. Those are good things, but they are not the essential thing. Transformation is simply a miracle: the incarnation and maturing of the Spirit of God within us.

Without the incarnation, *we cannot look like Him.*

We like things we can earn. Things we can work for. Things we can purchase, win, or even take by force. We like things we can accomplish and tasks we can control and complete. But looking like Him doesn't come by work or force. It comes through surrender. Growing up, I believed the concept of surrender to be a win/lose situation. I lose, and God wins. I'm giving up what I want so that God can have what He wants. If we see surrender with this mindset, we will never fully experience it. What if we choose to see this surrender for what it really is: a win/win?

Remember the imagery of the flattened ceiling? There is a great scene in Star Wars where Luke, Princess Leia, and Han Solo are trying to escape from a garbage compactor. The walls press in on them and the tension mounts, until at the very last second they are able to get out before being crushed. This scene is an apt depiction of our moment in history, courtesy of the secular age. We are being crushed, and the truth of the incarnation is being flattened.

The counter-whisper of the cave finds some traction here. If the incarnation can be relegated to the realm of myth and fantasy, Christianity is reduced to a mere natural religion. The teachings of Jesus would remain and may, at first glance, appear easy to hold onto, but divorced from their supernatural root they become a crushing weight upon us. Without the indwelling of the Spirit, we are not capable of loving *as He loved* and living *as He lived*. Imitation is not what we were created for.

Incarnation changes everything.

The House of Your Soul
Think of the strange, beautiful, and unsettling invitation that Mary heard. We have been given the same invitation.

The miracle in and of itself is strange, but even more mysterious is that Perfect Love chooses to place His life in us. How can this be? Not only that the Numen *could* make his life in us but that he *would* ... and why? Why would Perfect Love choose to make a home in such an imperfect place?

Perhaps this question reveals how much there is to learn about the nature of the Wholly Other and the wonder of Perfect Love. The real question is not about why Perfect Love would choose to make a home in us, but why *wouldn't* He? How quickly we forget who we are. We are His creatures! The work of His hands! His children! We are Perfect Love's fearfully and wonderfully made temples, designed to be inhabited and to be filled with the glory of God. Where else would He go? He is not a God who lives in houses built with human hands. *We are His house.*

The first home that Cammie and I lived in was built the year I was born – 1977. As we did our initial walk through, each room became more interesting than the one before. The house was complete with Garden of Eden wallpaper ... everywhere. The bathroom contained an oversized, mustard yellow jacuzzi tub with a metallic-silver painted mural of Adam and Eve in the nude. It was a sight to behold. Despite all of this, we loved it. Even from a distance we could see the good, the potential. It had a view of the mountains, mature trees, space to entertain, and a downstairs apartment.

We loved it enough to purchase it, Eden wallpaper and all. Of course, it needed some transformation. There were parts that were broken in, and other parts that were just broken. The roof had soft spots and there were drainage issues. The plastic, tulip light fixtures in the kitchen were so old that pieces broke off when we tried to clean them. The sagging concrete steps that greeted us at the front door didn't even make it on our seven-year to-do list. With a little love though, the house on Liberty Street was given new life. And as our love inhabited that space, life and beauty filled it. It became a place of laughter and joy, reflecting the love that purchased it and dwelt there. But it wasn't until we purchased it and *made our home there* that it began to transform. Our daughter was born there. We hosted little concerts in the backyard, dinners with energetic college students, and all sorts of gatherings. While the house remained a child of the 70's, it had new parents and it slowly began to reflect our image.

Imitation can take place from a distance, but transformation comes when our lives are purchased, and a new Spirit occupies the house.

Hope of Glory

With three words of surrender - *may it be* - everything about Mary's life changed. She was no longer alone at the center. Her life was no longer her own. She became a dwelling place for the life of the Wholly Other. Surrender opened the door to the mystery and the miracle of Christ in her.

Paul writes of a mystery that has been kept "secret for generations",[41] one that was revealed by the fullness of the Word of God (Jesus). He writes, "And this is the secret: Christ lives in you. This gives you assurance of sharing his glory."[42]

This is a mystery indeed, one that eluded many at the time of Jesus and has continued to evade Christian leaders throughout the centuries.

Christ in us, the hope of glory.

Christ in us, the hope of glory.

The miracle of new birth is that Christ makes His home in us. Not by power, not by might, but by His Spirit.[43] If we do not understand or are unwilling to start with the miracle, we will never experience the ultimate reality of transformation. We may know religion. We may even love it and be good at it. We may even imitate Christ ... but that is not our design. Our design is to look just like Him. Our design is to reflect His likeness and for Him to be incarnated within us.

> *So all of us who have had that veil removed can see and reflect the glory of the Lord. And the Lord—who is the Spirit—makes us more and more like him as we are changed into his glorious image.*[44]

For so long, I didn't understand any of this. I thought my efforts towards transformation were aimed at reflecting the "God out there." That seemed impossible. I had no idea that it was never about emulating the "God out there." It was always about cultivating a love for and relationship with the "God in here." The God that has chosen to dwell within the house of my soul! The indestructible seed of life will not return void. It will grow and flourish at the rate by which I allow it to do so. But in order for Christ in me to come alive, I must surrender. I must die to myself so that the new life may expand.

We were created to look just like Him. To be inhabited and animated by Perfect Love. This process begins with a miracle. Our invitation is to believe, and to surrender to it. Surrender isn't a religious discipline. It is the unsettled, fearful, and wonder-filled response of the creature to the Creator that says, *I believe… may it be.* It is a particular and yet continual point on this loop of life to the full. We refresh our surrender each day, each hour, each moment as we invite Him to increase as we decrease.

May it be: perhaps the most powerful, unknown, and misunderstood part of the good news. Christ in us, the hope of glory.

CHAPTER EIGHT

Nurture

We've got this gift of love, but love is like a precious plant.
You can't just accept it and leave it in the cupboard
or just think it's going to get on by itself.
You've got to keep watering it.
You've got to really look after it and nurture it.

John Lennon

When we say *may it be*, we invite the process and the posture of surrender. The story is no longer about us; the story is now about Christ *in* us. We are a part of *that* story. We are becoming Love, starting from the inside out. Our responsibility is to nurture a life that we did not create. Something is growing within us, and we must care for it.

Once we understand the miracle of Christ in us, nurture makes all the sense in the world. When we say yes to the incarnation, every circumstance is an opportunity to nurture the love growing within us. We become conscious that God is maturing Perfect Love in us.

If we skip the miracle, this process can feel like an instruction book of religious and spiritual practices. The Christian faith calls it discipleship, but without the incarnation it can feel like a collection of disconnected and disparate spiritual activities. Apart from a relationship with the Creator, disciplines often become harsh treatments of the mind and body. Holiness takes on a pious air and we have no sense of a true hunger and thirst for the word of God. I have felt this disconnection acutely at times in my life. Many of my conversations with people who are stuck and hopeless center around this precise issue.

When the incarnation and maturing of Christ in us is not the central purpose of our spiritual growth, our disciplines suffer and become disconnected from the goal. We're doing things, but they are not connected to *the* thing. Imagine cleaning your house, when what you're really trying to do is to tell your children how much you love them. Cleaning is a great activity, but without deliberate investment into your relationship with your children, the act of cleaning will never communicate the depth of your love. It is a discipline disconnected from the goal. When we understand our real relationship to the Creator within us, we can then participate in the work of nurturing that life.

Pregnant

The Spirit of the Numen has been incarnated in the very house of our soul. His life is *within* us. We become expectant; quite literally we are pregnant with His life, purpose, possibility, and beauty. Our restless posture suddenly shifts to a posture of hope. He has come. He is at home in us.

Finally … we get it, and we are starting to have it.

A sense of responsibility wells up within us as we experience the loss of our own life in preference of another. There is perhaps no greater, no more significant, no more sacred experience than nurturing this life within us.

But it's only true if it's true.

I remember when my wife, Cammie, was pregnant with our first daughter. As a man, I cannot fully speak to the human experience of pregnancy. Of course, I have witnessed the process as much as a husband and father can. I remember the first time I held the book *What to Expect When You're Expecting*. I looked at the cover, felt the pages, and wondered about the reality of a new person in the world. I spoke to that life, and I sang to that life. I guarded that life jealously.

But nothing compares to the transformation

that took place in my wife as she nurtured a life within her. She was the same and yet completely different. She was no longer the center. Our life together was recalibrated. Our interests and our loves were reordered. Old affections fell away as the healthy cultivation of this new life grew. Our present existence was wedded to the future in a brand new way. Choices about body, food, sleep, work, paint, soap, and *everything* were all on the table. Our pleasures, passions, and pursuits were transformed by the presence of a new life within my wife. This reality transformed our thinking, acting, and feeling.

Imagine this same sort of change happening spiritually as we nurture the life of Christ incarnated within us.

Christ in us, the hope of glory.

The Nature of Nurture

Like Mary as she received the incarnation of Christ, there are ways we are passive in this process. Jesus is the first mover. Apart from Him there would be no life to cultivate. We cannot manufacture any part of this on our own. But also, like Mary, there are ways in which we are very much involved and active in the process. We surrender to it, which is a conscious and powerful choice. Then, we nurture it. Remember, our part is to nurture a life that we didn't create but are responsible to.

To be the venue where love is produced is a

beautiful thing. The seed of mature love is birthed in us, poised to grow from infancy to maturity. So what does our responsibility look like as the process unfolds within us?

Scripture teaches us many things about what transformed lives look like. It urges us to remain in the light and warns against any activity that will grieve the Spirit of God within us. It encourages holiness and prayer, community and communion, worship and study, fasting and silence. Making the choice to do these things is a very important part of the process of nurture. But it is not the only part. We can't be trying to cultivate mature, selfless love while at the same time feeding selfish love. The other changes we must make involve putting down the activities that do not nurture the Spirit of Christ in us.

And yet all these changes – picking up the healthy habits and putting down the unhealthy ones – do not fully encapsulate the process of nurture. It is not simply staying away from sinful things and submerging our life in pure and holy things that changes us to look like Jesus. It is *creating and cultivating the environment* in which He can come alive within us. It is nurturing the relationship with Him that will allow this life to flourish.

The pregnancy analogy continues to help us understand this in a new way. Ideally, a pregnant woman should get rest, eat well, and take care of her body. She also knows that she should avoid things like drugs, alcohol, and smoking. As I said, all of our priorities and decisions were reordered when Cammie was pregnant. This was not because we believed that doing all these things would *create* a child within her. No. The child was already there. We made the choices to create and cultivate the environment so that that child could grow.

This is the nature of nurture.

Restless and Reckless

I drive so slowly, it makes my kids crazy.

Dad, speed up! Dad, come on!

I hear it all the time. But I wasn't always this way. The presence of those lives in the car with me has completely changed my attitude toward driving.

There is a particularly winding, sloping section of Highway 101 that runs along the Oregon coast, just north of a little town called Lincoln City. In my reckless, alone-in-the-center days I loved finding that stretch of road and pushing the very outer limits of speed that I thought I could control. I actually remember one time pushing a little beyond my control, and that felt even better. I was careless because I wasn't concerned for anyone but myself. That would never take place if someone else I loved was in the car, much less a life that I was responsible to nurture and care for.

I have met people who have basically stopped

trying, hoping, or believing that transformation will come. They received Christ, but never chose the process of nurture. Instead of transformation, there was only a continual pursuit of self-love. Formerly, I walked this path. I indulged in all manner of things. When I look back, I see almost a decade of my life where I lived in what now seems like such a strange and sad place. I was restless and so reckless. I think I was driving at 100 miles per hour in almost every area of my life. Within me was a seed, pregnant with the potential to transform my life. I was longing for it but somehow, even after growing up in the church, my vision had never turned in. I had never really understood that there was a life within me and was therefore unaware of my responsibility to nurture it.

When I finally realized that there was another life residing within the house of my soul, I felt a deep sense of sadness and regret. It was something like a woman not discovering she is pregnant until late in the third trimester. If she hasn't known about the life within her, if she hasn't been taking care of her body, it will be a weighty discovery. If there have been drinking and smoking, late nights and stressful days, that moment will take on enormous significance. Things that didn't seem to matter before the pregnancy was known suddenly mean everything.

I felt something akin to this when I came to the realization that it was never about the "God out there," but always about the "God in here." I realized that Christ in me was the hope of glory – not my glory but *His* glory. Christ in me was the living, breathing manifestation of the gospel, the embodiment of shalom.

What had I been doing with it all these years?

Christ had been hidden inside me. My immature, selfish love had led me into spaces, relationships, and habits that were absolutely harmful to the formation of His life in me. The whole time I avoided things like prayer, studying scripture, habits of adoration and worship, time in community, and caring for my inward life. I didn't need any of that stuff. I didn't want any of that stuff. I didn't enjoy it. I was conscious of no other life in me, and so I behaved accordingly.

The process of nurture truly began for me when I realized that I didn't need to do those things just for *me*. I needed to do them for *Him*. I was learning to prefer another over myself, learning to prefer the practices and patterns that are needed to nurture that life within me. I began to choose actions that would allow Him to flourish, for me to decrease so that He might increase.

The shame surrounding this newly revealed "pregnancy" was swallowed up by wonder. Fear and regret diminished as my understanding of the depth of His grace, patience, and love grew. I became overwhelmingly grateful for the sweet reality that there is nothing I can do to be separate from the Perfect Love that had made its life in me. I may have been damaging my own life and the hearts of those around me, I may have been grieving the Father, but the indestructible seed was still waiting within. He remained with me through all those years of restless and reckless behavior, through all of the hollow spaces, broken relationships, and detrimental habits. His life was there, grieving and unloved, yet patient and pursuing.

When I finally grasped it, when I finally understood the pregnant state of my soul, I couldn't go back. The things that I legitimately loved suddenly became less important in light of the life within. And, little by little, evidence of a new life began to appear.

Infancy to Maturity

Here's a radical thought: some of the things we *think* are nurturing to the life of Christ within us are actually *not nurturing at all.*

Most parents these days put an exorbitant amount of time, money, and effort into acquiring the requisite 137 plus items that "every good parent" should have for their newborn. We are led to believe that these provide a "nurturing" environment for a new baby – swings and scales and lights and music and wraps and toys and clothes and blankets. And not just any sorts of these items – the *best* sorts of these items. Time is poured into creating the perfect nursery, with the most calming paint color, music, décor, and more. But is this nurture? Are these truly the essential things? No. Not really. These things are nice. They reflect love. They make us feel more confident as parents. But what does the baby truly need to grow? Food. Sleep. Love. That's it. So often, we expend energy on things that don't provide any sort of true nurture whatsoever.

I think we see this same misguidance in our religious practice and even in the church. We spend loads of time and money on things that do not nurture the life within us. Our high power, high octane, or even sometimes highly liturgical environments throw all sorts of things at the crowds. Are liturgies or fog machines or kids' programs or rock bands or small groups *bad*? No. Not at all. Not on their own. But if we believe that simply attending or acquiring those things provides any nurture to the life of Christ within us, we are missing something pretty huge. If the church is not inviting the crowds to understand that they are pregnant with a new life inside of them, then these practices won't matter. It's like giving the baby a fancy, thousand-dollar stroller when all the baby really needs is milk, and sleep, and to be held.

In all honesty, we might have to admit that much of what we have asked the church for isn't nurturing. Cultivating a life is more than demanding well-run programs and phenomenal music. The practices that are truly nurturing, like the contemplative practices of hearing and digesting the scriptures, or being still and silent and listening, are often seen as rather boring. The cave has shaped us for distraction and entertainment, and its counter-whisper points us toward them. Instead of judging an activity or initiative in terms of "cool" or "boring," the essential question we should ask is: *what nurtures the life of Christ within us?* What habits, practices, disciplines, or activities bring love to maturity? Do those and nothing else.

So how do we do that?

Remember the source. The point of reference. The man, Jesus. God became flesh and dwelt among us. He came and paid the price for sin so that relationship could be restored. He came so that He could dwell with us and within us. He came so that we could catch a vision of who *we* are created to be: just like Him.

Jesus was a radical. He ate with sinners. He touched lepers. He exulted children and honored and respected women. He walked slowly and retreated in prayer. He spoke patiently to His motley crew of disciples. He cooked food for people and cleaned up after them. He forgave those who betrayed him. He blessed those who cursed his name. He spoke Truth when it was not welcome. He blew past cultural barriers and religious norms and demonstrated mature love even when it was costly, even to the point of offering his own life on a cross. We are nurturing *that* life within us.

Christ in us, the hope of glory.

Long, Slow, and Deep

Nurturing is about moving from surrender to the active participation of developing love as it moves from infancy to maturity. We care for the seed of mature love by removing things that are oriented towards self-love. We hold ourselves in the tension between all things being permissible, and the knowledge that some things may harm the maturing love within us. We ask ourselves what practices and habits are best for cultivating life to the full.

This takes an awareness that builds over time. We won't "get it right" in the beginning, and that's okay. The process is meant to take a lifetime. As we participate in it, we begin to discover that true nurture is less about the spiritual activities we are doing and more about our reason for doing them.

For example, choosing to read our Bibles, praying, and journaling do not necessarily connect to the process of love maturing in us. If we are doing these things to check a box, or to fulfill our own selfish needs for meditation and solitude, then that isn't quite the same thing as doing those things with the intent to nurture the life within us. And so, we learn to ask Him to guide us, to help us pay attention to the process of nurture.

God, how are you maturing your love within me?

In the beginning of this process we can be desperate, disconnected, distracted, and all over the map. We might find ourselves flexing our moral muscle rather than remembering it's about the nurture of the seed within us. We might catch ourselves pushing rather than choosing patience. We might see ourselves trying rather than cultivating. So, we simply notice, and then choose to return to the place of nurture.

Long, slow, and deep. That's how it works. Mind you, this is the antithesis of how our culture says things work. But stay the course, friend, in spite of the culture around us. The trajectory of short, fast, and shallow is very different than that of long, slow and deep. As love grows within us, we become conscious of the process. We learn to examine ourselves, and we expect to live differently based on our sensitivity to His Spirit. This takes time, and we learn to celebrate every part of the journey.

Vision Up becomes Vision In. Christ becomes the center of our worship and the center of our lives. Everything begins to be a venue for the maturing of His Love – our jobs, our marriages, our parenting, our travel, our hobbies, our churches, our suffering, our weakness, our pain, our joy – all of it. Flourishing is relational not circumstantial. We're in relationship with the life of Christ within us. In the quietness of private moments, we look upon that life and say, *may you increase, and may I decrease.*

We embrace the long, slow, deep process and all that it means. Nurturing the life of love in us means change. It means preferring another over ourselves. It means maturity. And it is a process that continues until His life in us is fully revealed.

CHAPTER NINE

Transformation

Dear friends, we are already God's children,
but he has not yet shown us what we will be like when
Christ appears.
But we do know that we will be like him, for we will see
him as he really is.

1 John 3:2 NLT

Here we are, at the final vantage point of Vision In. In the last section, Vision Up, we walked the path of looking up: seeing Jesus face to face, confessing that He is God, and the *response* of adoration. In this section, Vision In, we walk the path of looking in: surrendering to Him, nurturing the new life within us, and the *response* of transformation. We cannot look to Him and remain the same. If we allow Christ to come into our lives, if we nurture that new life within us, we cannot be other than transformed, completely and utterly changed. We do not bring about this transformation; we simply participate in it.

Attempting to write about transformation is a tricky thing. Volumes have been written on transformation in Christ. Amazing contributions have been authored on spiritual direction, spiritual formation, and sanctification. What can possibly be added? If I have anything important to add to the conversation, it is this: real transformation, looking more like Jesus, does not come about by strength, might, or intellectual capacity. Consequently, it is not something we try for. *It is something we die for.* And that is beautiful, powerful, scandalous news.

I don't have a new technique to share about spiritual formation, but rather a testimony of a life. I testify to the fact that we were created to be in relationship with Him, and that this relationship changes us. It transforms us. This is good news for people like me.

Adoration leads to transformation. It's generative. It opens the door to a new life that flows from and is connected to the deep history and mystery of the Christian faith. We do not fashion ourselves into His image. Any attempt to do so violates the Creator/creature relationship. His image is worked out from within. The lifting of false expectations of production or performance allows us to experience a light burden of learning to nurture a life we didn't create. We are responsible *to* a life we are not responsible *for*.

Letting Go

We make the choice to surrender, and engage the long, slow, and deep process of nurture. If the response to these things is transformation, then what is it that must transform? It is not only about the things that come alive in us… *it is also about the things that must die in us.* Transformation requires a look in the mirror to see the parts of our image that do not reflect His love and that need to diminish. To be honest, I have to sit with this for a minute. Some of the parts of myself that I know need to diminish are, frankly, parts that I have come to love. They have been around for so long that it would be hard, even strange, to see them go. There are certain parts of me that *others* need me to be. I am a pleaser. I hold onto these things because I don't want to feel the rejection of others. That's hard to admit, but it's the truth.

When I turn the mirror and allow these parts of me to be illuminated, it's hard to entertain the notion that they need to disappear. It feels pretty threatening. I am a future thinker, but in many ways, I am afraid of the unknown. *What if I let these parts of me go? What if I begin to nurture and reflect love and end up getting hurt or misunderstood?* When I traverse the deep places of my identity where fear, pride, lust, power, and self-protection still roam and dominate the landscape, it is sometimes very difficult for me to let them go. Indeed, I can become dependent on these things, finding comfort in the familiarity of what is predictable.

The parts of us that need to diminish will stay put as long as we continue to look to them either in adoration or fear. It is a losing battle. They will not go until we hunger and thirst for the image of Perfect Love to be restored in us. Until our love for Him is greater than our love for or fear of our dark places, we will keep looking back, and we will continue to reflect those parts of our own image out into the world.

Transformation means letting go. We are no longer slaves to ourselves, because we have allowed our true selves to be cultivated from the seed of Christ in us. We are set free from the fear of losing our identity, so we gladly lay down our life in favor of the real life within us. Our adolescent loves no longer consume us, because Perfect Love has begun to change our tastes, our desires, our vision, our longings, our affections. Transformation is loving *His* life in us more than our own version of our life.

I'm Gonna Be Like You

Perhaps the clearest vision of transformational love is the story of the prodigal son.[45] This parable describes the journey of a young man who rebels against his father, declares that he is essentially done with him, takes his entire inheritance, and then throws it all away in wild living. When the cash runs out and he comes to the end of himself, he recognizes that even his father's hired hands have it better than he does. The young son returns home in shame, but before he reaches the house his father runs to greet him. The father joyfully restores his son to his place in the family and throws a party in his honor. This is not an easy pill to swallow for the older brother who has been faithfully working at home the whole time. He feels cheated and is angry that his father would extend grace, mercy, and resources to the younger brother.

If we are honest, we can say that we identify with both the younger and older brother at different moments in our lives, and we can learn important things from both characters. Sometimes we are prideful, like the older brother, wanting honor and working to earn the love of our father. Sometimes we are selfish, like the younger brother, burning our resources until they are spent and then picking up a load of shame.

However, there is an element beyond the older/younger brother dynamic. The real wonder at the center of this parable is *the father*. He loves *both* of his sons; they have his DNA. They were created in *his* image. The father's love draws them close with the gentleness and skill of a potter's hand, longing to shape them both with his grace. His desire for them is not only that they would experience his love, but that his love would transform them.

As Henri Nouwen says, "Becoming like the heavenly Father is not just one important aspect of Jesus' teaching, it is the very heart of his message."[46] Transformation in Christ is not becoming a better version of ourselves. Our destiny is to look like our Father. I can hear it in the haunting verse from Harry Chapin's song, *Cat's in the Cradle*. "I'm gonna be like you, Dad. You know I'm gonna be like you."[47]

I never considered that my destiny was to mature to look like the father in the story. I was so fixated on myself as being the elder brother or younger brother that I missed it. The gospel was good news, but only in the limited sense that I felt set free to kick back and enjoy the party as a forgiven son. I was alive but not full. I had yet to even begin to understand the profound implications that flow from Jesus' words, "Anyone who has seen Me has seen the Father."[48] I had not yet engaged the transformational nature imbedded in His words, "I am in my Father, and you are in me, and I am in you."[49]

Transformation comes with the letting go. Both sons in the story must let go in order to begin to look like the father. The younger brother is full of guilt and shame and fear, but those things diminish in the transforming power of the father's love. The older brother is full of pride and the sense of his own self, but this can also diminish in the wake of the father's love. Imagine the freedom, the joy, the wholeness that would come for those brothers if they chose to let go of the fear and pride and simply receive the powerful love of the father. Imagine if they allowed themselves to begin to look like him.

Your Debt Has Been Paid

In my younger days, I resembled the prodigal son. I was a young man, living in a loft apartment in Oregon. It was a good spot. The only downside to the apartment, however, was the on-street parking spot located directly below my apartment. It was almost always available when I needed it, so there was no hiding the fact that I was home. In addition to my car being out front, I had four large windows that overlooked the street. If I wasn't careful, I could almost make eye contact with anyone walking on the sidewalk or driving in the right lane. All that to say, when my mom knocked on my door one Easter morning, there was no way to pretend that I wasn't home.

I wasn't thrilled by the knock, and I became even less thrilled when I looked out the peephole and saw my mom standing there. The building was built in 1906 and the floors were original wood, so not only had she seen my car parked smack dab on the street, she could also hear that I was standing on the other side of the door. Maybe that's why she looked so uncomfortable. Imagine the prodigal son at the end of his revelry. Now imagine him looking outside to see his mom or dad standing there. I couldn't avoid her, and I certainly had no desire to speak to her. I had burned every bridge and spent every last ounce of grace I could possibly have deserved.

I opened the door just enough to position myself directly in the gap. Honestly, I had no idea what to say. The only thing that came out of my mouth was, "Hi."

She handed me a small white envelope, wished me a Happy Easter, and then turned around and walked down the hall. I retreated inside and looked down at her beautiful handwriting on the front. *Happy Easter*. That was it. That was all it said. That, and a little signature flower she always draws on outgoing mail. I opened the envelope, and inside was a card with a handwritten note that simply said, "Your debt has been paid, Happy Easter." And just like that, my parents forgave an entire financial loan that I owed them in order to help me undo the knots I had tied myself up with.

Years prior they had loaned me money for school, and I had never paid them back. Not because I couldn't, but just because I hadn't. I was so self-absorbed. I had the means to reconcile the debt, but I took license with their grace. I was thriving in my career, had a great apartment and a great car – but I was not in relationship with them. My parents continued to pursue me, and I continued to brush them off. I wouldn't come to them, and so they came to me. Mature love walked into my adolescent love and overwhelmed me with a mercy I didn't deserve. When my mom stood there that day, and I awkwardly barricaded the doorway, all that was behind me was destruction, embarrassment, shame, and selfishness. And all that was in front of me was grace, forgiveness, and love.

I, the prodigal son, had been forgiven.

Not just forgiven but embraced. Pursued. Loved.

There is a scripture that speaks of the highest display of God's love being poured out on our behalf "while we were still sinners."[50] In the midst of our brokenness, the Life that had become a home for Perfect Love was broken to make us whole. We are transformed to reflect *this* Love. This is the love that my mother showed me that day.

I didn't seek my mom out that morning, nor did my parents simply decide to call and tell me the good news from a distance. Their words became flesh in a real and costly demonstration of their love. Their love stooped low, found me in my mess, and joined me in my brokenness in order to release me from my debt. Their love for me was transformational.

Their love kindled a desire within me to reflect it back to them.

Mature Love

The father of the prodigal son displays mature love. It is a love that transforms each son and daughter to resemble the Father. Mature love is filled with delight: it sees the good first and celebrates it. Mature love is not indifferent to brokenness: it does not recoil or retreat from it, but rather moves toward brokenness with compassion. Mature love is seasoned with hope: it sees the redemptive version of the future and chooses to walk into it.

Although I desire to see love mature in me, it is not without struggle. The child in me, the adolescent love in me, still sings a much darker and more self-absorbed rendition of the old Toys "R" Us jingle: "I don't want to grow up, because if I did, I wouldn't be a Toys 'R' Us kid." I feel that struggle. There is a battle between a love within me destined to mature, and a flesh and bone child still too selfish to grow up.

In some ways I think my selfishness is actually a mask for fear. A more honest assessment might be that I'm afraid to see love fully mature because I'm not ready to say goodbye to the prodigal son in me. There is still a part of me that wants *him* at the center. It's who others know me to be, the me I am comfortable introducing and have spent a lifetime defending. It's the identity I know, and frankly I fear losing it.

However, if I chose to let it go, something else could take its place, a kind of love that is patient and kind. Love that is not envious, boastful or proud, that does not dishonor others. Love that is not self-seeking, nor easily angered.

Mature love keeps no record of wrongs. It does not delight in evil but rejoices with the truth.

Mature love always protects, always trusts, always hopes and always perseveres.

Mature love never fails.[51]

Broken and Redeemed

If we skip this movement, if we bypass the daily decision of letting go, we might still "get" it. Transformation is understandable. *We will get it, but we will not have it.* We will never experience transformation without a relationship with the Father that chooses to release our old selves in favor of our true selves. Transformation invites us to die to the right to control something that we seized control of, something we didn't build, something that has since been broken: ourselves.

It is a joy to see and experience the designer, the giver of life, enter and affirm what's good. There is no one with a deeper understanding of our broken places than Him. When the Creator pauses in those places, he remembers them whole. He understands why and how they were broken. God remembers. Those parts of us are not glossed over or ignored. Brokenness in our lives matters to the Creator. He understands. He weeps. And then he sees and brings about transformation. The Father embraces the son with the hope of the future with full restoration and redemption. Scripture says that He "brings the dead back to life and creates new things out of nothing."[52]

Joy. Life. Hope.

Imagine the Creator of the universe creating those things within you.

The greatest obstacle to transformation in my life was *me*. My vision of God was too small and my vision of myself was too great. I was not ready to look like Him until I realized that only by bearing Love's image could I truly love someone else the way that they deserved to be loved. To fully love God and fully love others, I needed Love to dwell in me.

Remember the renovation project of our Liberty Street 70's home? We were facing all sorts of exterior damage and decay, interior disrepair, and a cracked foundation. But we chose to restore and redeem the broken places of that home. It's the same way with our souls in the process of transformation. There are late night renovations to our hearts, long weekends of hard work, and needed days of rest. There are gentle days of decoration and there are "demo" days that cut to the core. I've learned that some of the difficult experiences and seasons that I face are simply part of this transformative, metamorphic process.

But in all of it, we are never alone. In the spiritual sense, *we* are not remodeling the house. The Father is. He purchased it. He dwells in it. His presence and love will transform it. We are invited to participate in His work as we stay close to Him.

As we do, we discover more of who He is, and how He sees. We learn more about who we are and who we are created to be. What a gift. We get to invest time alongside the Creator, listening as He celebrates the good things about us that only He knows, the secret things, the hidden elements of design that were covered up, undervalued, and refashioned for other things. We get to rest as he shows us the broken parts, some of which we didn't even know were broken. How could we? It takes the designer Himself to be present, and to help us understand the ways He ordered us, the ways that He created us to flourish and experience life to the full. We find hope again as He reveals to us a future of becoming more like Him.

Transformation is a *miracle*.

Vision Up becomes Vision In becomes Vision Out.

As we look to Him, we can say with full assurance, "I'm gonna be like you, Dad. You know I'm gonna be like you."

Section Four

Vision Out

Noticing

The world around me is the same,
Yet completely different.
I see through the eyes of mature love. I slow my pace.
My breath.
My life.
There is much to see that I missed before.
Moment by moment,
I notice the good, and I affirm it.
I notice the broken, and I acknowledge it.
I notice the future, and I agree with the coming shalom.
Good. Broken. Future.
All three. Always.
Now I see.

Embrace

It is not enough to notice.
I long to embrace, just like my Father.
I affirm the good and celebrate.
I acknowledge the broken and mourn.
I participate with the future and mend.
I delight in shalom.
I travel the seams where things are being set right again.
I lean in close, present and patient.
Fear dies as love comes fully alive.
Life to the full.
My life is full.
Now I see.

Love

The Source of Love is alive in me.
My Love flows into the margins and the seams.
I am emptied.
I am poured out.
My Love returns to the Source.
I am filled anew.
My heart steadies with
Gratitude
Compassion
Hope.
He is love. I am love. They are loved.
Now I see.

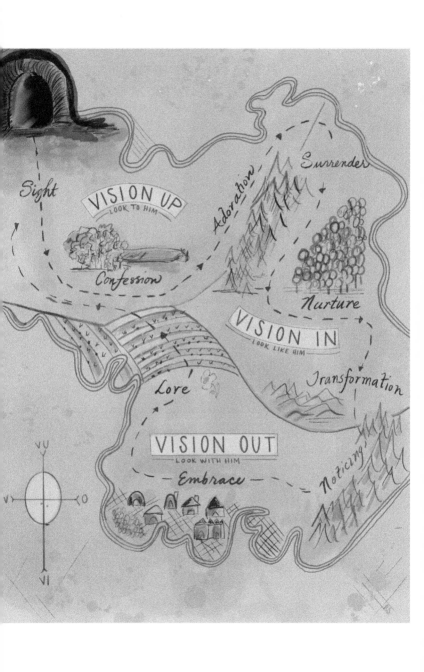

CHAPTER TEN

Noticing

When we can see the image of God
where we don't want to see the image of God,
then we see with eyes not our own.

Richard Rohr

We walk towards love; always love. When our vision is up, we look *to* Him and love Him back with adoration. When our vision is in, we look *like* Him and experience His love in transformation. Now, we look *with* Him, returning love into his world. Vision Out begins with learning to notice who, what, and how the Creator sees.

This new scenic viewpoint on our trail opens our eyes in a whole new way. Little by little, as love matures within us, we begin to see the world differently. Our old way was oriented towards scarcity and failure. Our old way was colored by fear. Our old way was rushed and saw mostly what was on the exterior of things. Our old way was selfish and immature.

Mature love is different. It sees in sequence and depth: the good, the broken, and the future. It is oriented towards abundance and hope. Mature love slows down to notice more than a façade; it sees *truth*, and delights in it. This noticing doesn't happen merely because we choose to see things differently. It happens because of our relationship to the people in our lives, and to the Creator. Perfect Love draws us out of the cave and into relationship, where life is flourishing and full.

We rediscover how to notice the good, the broken, and the future. In this discovery we realize that life is full. So full! Life is brimming over with things to celebrate. Life is also full of suffering and things to hope for. We share laughter, tears, dreams, and love with those around us. We didn't do this in the cave! We didn't even notice.

In the simple children's book, *Brown Bear, Brown Bear, What Do You See?*, the very question is asked, "What do you see?"[53]

The question we need to ask ourselves is, "Mature love, mature love, what do you see?" I ask that question many times a day. When I feel my anxiety, my fear, or my defensiveness pulling me into the posture of the cave, I slow down and ask myself this question.

What does mature love see?

Commingled

Life is complicated. If you don't believe me, look through someone's garbage. This is not a metaphor. I used to do this as part of my work collecting evidence for a narcotics task force. My job was to look for drugs and other illegal substances in other people's garbage. It was an eye-opening assignment. As I rummaged through the trash of suspected dealers, I also found Barbie coloring book pages filled in with pink crayon, receipts for diapers and formula, leftover food, old mail, pictures, toy packaging, credit card statements… and other things that were never intended for someone else to see. Kneeling on a tarp covered in garbage, I learned that the good guys are not all good and the bad guys are not all bad. Life is far more complicated than it appears.

Mature love requires a commingled perspective.

My days collecting evidence also included forensic photography. One foggy October morning, I stood under a small awning of an office building in my quiet, Oregon hometown. I was there to photograph a crime scene and collect the pieces of a life ended too soon. On the ground next to me was a blood-covered sleeping bag, from which the body of a dead man had recently been removed. I will never forget him. He was a man without a home who lived and died on the streets. Two men attacked him while he slept and beat him to death for the money from his social security check.

When I went home that day, my heart broke and I couldn't keep back the tears. They flowed from a place beyond conscious sadness, a deeper place where the hurt just overwhelms. My work felt pointless and hopeless, a mere drop in the bucket. There was too much violence, too much hatred, too much selfishness, too much pain in this world. I could see *nothing* beyond the brokenness, and it left me devastated. I couldn't find a commingled perspective. I couldn't see anything good.

This was not mature love.

We crave straight lines and simple math. When life reveals someone as broken, we often choose not to see the good. Our perspective tells us that we know exactly where they belong, and we are happy to keep them there. We might fear them or hate them, run and hide from them, oppose them or even kill them. It's much easier to push the broken aside or put the broken away. Often, we do this even to ourselves. Brokenness disgusts us.

If we are never unsettled by the reflection of the Numen in our enemy, we remain unloving. If we refuse to recognize the dignity in strangers, they are easy to ignore. If we run from our own brokenness, we'll never truly be free of the cave. When we don't see possibility of wholeness, it's easier to let the broken things go.

Mature love's vision is commingled.

The good, the broken, and the future.

All three, always.

One of the most respectful young men I have ever known was a high school student when I met him. He sold drugs to help his mom take care of his young sisters. *Commingled.* I once sat at a table across from a highly successful businessman who had everything: the mansion, the boat, the second home, the luxury cars, the vacations. As I listened, he shared how his obsession with his work had broken his marriage and family. *Commingled.* I know pastors who struggle with suicidal thoughts and cops who have broken the law. I've met high performing students who are homeless and privileged kids who are running away. *Commingled.*

Commingled and complicated.

Vision Out invites us to resist the temptation of trying to "flatten" our enchanted story, even if it would make things less complicated. Mature love sees the good, the broken and the future, always present in all things, always commingled. It sees with the eyes of the Creator, the Father, the Redeemer.

Noticing the Good

I have met so many people who seem to have lost the ability to notice the good in our created world. This is a devastating way to share life together. If we can't notice the good first, the whole dance is off. We step on people's feet, we get tripped up, and everyone gets hurt. The most common response I hear from folks who want to push back on this point is that we live in a fallen world and so everything is broken. Well, yes, that's true. All of creation is broken ... but it is also *good enough to redeem*. What if we were to first look for the good?

Psychologists use the term cognitive distortion to describe what happens when our minds get trapped in a pattern that sees and interprets data in harmful ways. In a similar way, if we remove the good as our starting place, our vision gets dark in a hurry. We begin to see our entire existence in distortion, taking in the things that are obviously broken without being able to perceive the commingled good. We base our assumptions and assessments on this distorted perspective, and then we are bewildered as to why everything looks so scary or pathetic. This starting point for interpretation harms interactions, destroys relationships, and demolishes joy.

We must start with the good.

When you enter into a situation – a meeting, your work place, a restaurant, a church, your home – breathe. Take two seconds to look and listen through the lens of mature love. Then affirm the good. Make a list, an inventory in your brain, of things that are very good. We're not moving to embrace it yet, just simply learning to notice. This is a discipline and an art that flows from the life and beauty of Christ maturing within us.

Unfortunately, although seeing the good first is simple, it's not easy. Habit. Harm. Experience. Bad theology. These all color the lens through which we see the world. We are conditioned to look with the eyes of consumers, cynics, critics, competitors, and skeptics, directed over and over by voices of accusation and despair that look only at brokenness. No beauty. No future. Add constant distraction to the mix, and we can understand why seeing the good first is such a struggle. As love matures it does get easier, but it still remains a choice. We choose to look with Him, moment by moment. We choose this love because of the overflow of Him *in* us.

The good is found in kindness in the classroom and mercy in the courts. It is found on the first night in a new home and on the last night on earth. It is justice for the oppressed and freedom for the captive. It is in the unseen hours spent loving a new life and the late-night hours of laughter shared with old friends. It is in the church and in the town square, in great halls and backyard stages.

What do you see *first* when you look at your home? Is it too big? Too small? Too old? Too new? What do you see *first* when you see your neighbors? Are they strange? Too old? Too strong? Too white? Too brown? Too religious? Not religious enough? What do we see first when we look at our communities? Our governments? Our politicians? What do we see *first* when we look at our friend, our enemy, our children, or our spouse?

What do we see *first* when we look in the mirror?

Some might argue that in our selfie-obsessed, narcissistic culture, advocating that we begin by seeing the good in ourselves is a recipe for disaster. But if we do not understand how to rightly recognize the good in ourselves, how can we recognize it anywhere else? Inability to see the good in creatures of the Creator brings harm to ourselves, others, and the One we were made by and for.

I am writing to remind you who you are, beloved children of the Most High God. You are *very good*. You have a unique capacity to reflect the image of God in a particular way, distinct from any other creature on this planet. You are beautiful, fearfully and wonderfully made with the marvelous ability to think, act, and feel. You are endowed with knowledge, expertise, creativity, and the capacity to shape and enrich the human experience. You are a dwelling place for Perfect Love and an instrument through which that love is expressed.

"Creature, creature, who do you see? Can you see who I made you to be?"

Can you hear the Voice of the Creator, inviting you to notice yourself and His world through His eyes of love?

We notice and affirm the good.

Noticing the Broken

The good exists. But, so does the broken. Loss, despair,

grief, and suffering are all around us and with us, every day. I am not suggesting that we become such optimists, looking for the good in everything, that we pretend broken things don't exist. I am also not suggesting that we distort truth too far in the other direction and find ourselves taking something that is wrong and calling it good. No. There is deep brokenness in this world, and we cannot turn a blind eye if we choose to see through the eyes of mature love.

How do we define brokenness?

Brokenness is a violation of shalom. Brokenness is the absence of flourishing, delight, and wholeness. It is what causes the gashes in the fabric of our universal covering, leaving large, gaping shreds of what was meant to be. It is the devastation that followed the separation of creatures from Creator. Sickness, injustice, poverty, hurt, violence, pollution, death. These things violate shalom. When we see the broken, we acknowledge it and say, that's not right.[54] *That's not right!*

We notice brokenness all around us, and certainly within us. When we see our own brokenness, we find ourselves praying that no one notices us while at the same time aching for someone to do just that. These are often the parts of the story that we ignore, consciously or unconsciously. Mature love doesn't ignore brokenness. It is not afraid of it or repulsed by it. It doesn't discard broken people, places, or things. It doesn't cheapen or dishonor hurt by pretending it is not there. It is precisely because it *can* notice the good that mature love can also notice the broken.

And notice, *we must.* An invitation to life to the full is not an invitation to a pain free life; it is an invitation to face pain honestly and unafraid. Facing headlong into the reality of brokenness through the lens of mature love gives us a hope that transcends the grave, setting us free from fear. We cannot be free until we stand at the threshold of deep brokenness - even our own mortality - and say: *Now I See.*

Now I see that I *am* broken, and I am unafraid to acknowledge it. I am no longer ashamed of it. No longer held hostage to it. No longer trying to create some theology to explain it or escape it. Once we truly see our brokenness, we can choose to endure suffering with courage and hope. Love continues to mature as we suffer in our own stories and come alongside suffering in the stories of those around us.

When we acknowledge the broken, we are not trying to fix it all or rush to make everything whole. Noticing brokenness simply recognizes reality and dignifies the hurting. When we attempt to conceal, ignore, or erase brokenness, we choose to conceal, ignore, or erase love. Our obsession with comfort makes it very difficult to face or give attention to things we can't fix. But there is no wholeness without dignity. And there is no dignity if we don't notice the broken. Noticing acknowledges worth, value, loss, pain, and truth.

We notice and acknowledge the broken.

Noticing the Future

I am a morning person, and I always have been. The older I get, the more I love it. Every dawn represents a new opportunity for life and beauty to appear. After living on the West Coast for almost forty years, I am now experiencing the opportunity to welcome the sunrise over the waters of the eastern horizon. I haven't done it yet, but I would love to sail into the Atlantic and watch the sun come up over the horizon, to see the first seconds of a new day. I want to experience life right there, right on that seam of evening and morning.

Shalom is the future, a new day.

Reconciliation is the seam, the moment when evening gives way to morning.

Picture the fabric of reality, shredded and torn by all that violates shalom. Can you see rips where the broken has invaded and disrupted the good? And then, can you also see how that fabric might yet be woven back together? Imagine a seam, woven into the fabric, mending the torn places with one stitch at a time. *That* is the vision of the future we participate in. Shalom restored, all things mended, all things woven together and whole.

Seams are the early evidence of things being set right. *Reconciliation is the early morning of shalom.* Everywhere we see reconciliation, we catch a glimpse of the future. Mature love looks for two things: seams already being woven together and seams in need of repair. Mature love is constantly scanning for and noticing new opportunities where shalom can appear, and scanning for new opportunities to witness the present woven into the future.

Mature love is expectant love.

> *And I heard a loud shout from the throne, saying, "Look, God's home is now among his people! He will live with them, and they will be his people. God himself will be with them. He will wipe every tear from their eyes, and there will be no more death or sorrow or crying or pain. All these things are gone forever."*
>
> *And the one sitting on the throne said, "Look, I am making everything new!"*[55]

No more tears. No more death. No more conflict. This is the future of shalom. Every single day it is appearing. Mature love expects shalom and is certain of it, *even when it can't be seen.* Having affirmed the good and acknowledged the broken, we look to the future. Where is there a possibility of making things whole and or setting things right? Where are the seams, the places where we notice the mending taking place?

Where we see a possibility to set things right, we say *yes*! We agree with and affirm the possibility of wholeness. We envision the space for redemption, and we recognize the hope inherent in every chapter of every story.

We notice and agree with the future.

Slowing Down

How do we learn to notice? To be honest, our pace of life is completely out of sync with giving good attention to anything. Noticing with the eyes of mature love takes time and discipline. It takes slowing down to learn to ask the question, "Mature love, what do you see?" Life to the full isn't on the race-track, the fast-track, or the road most traveled. Our current cultural pace of life is in *direct conflict* with noticing and frankly, with love. If we want life to the full in relationship with Jesus, then we walk at his pace.

Yes.

We walk.

Kosuke Koyama writes of this.

"Love has its speed. It is a spiritual speed. It is a different kind of speed from the technological speed to which we are accustomed. It goes on in the depth of our life, whether we notice or not, at three miles an hour. It is the speed we walk and therefore the speed the love of God walks."[66]

It is impossible to notice the true beauty of a bird or tree when traveling at 80 mph. It is impossible to notice the smile and wonder of a child when scrolling through Instagram. It is impossible to notice the smell and taste of dinner when we are cramming fast food down our throat. It is impossible to see the anxiety in your teenager's eyes when you aren't looking at them. When we choose to participate in the frenetic pace of our society, we miss life. We miss beauty.

Slow down.

Please.

I am saying this as much to myself as I am to you.

The Road to Hana in Maui is known for its elevations, mud slicks, switchbacks, waterfalls, and breathtaking views. In order to appreciate the drive, or really even to traverse it, you must down-shift and drive carefully. To discover the stunning wonder of the island, you have to take *this* road that is long and slow. If you look at the island's edge, you only get a small glimpse of what is truly at the heart of this magnificent place; it is the slow, curving, meandering road that reveals the greatest beauty.

Slow down.

Perhaps there are times in our life where circumstances slow us down. We might initially find ourselves overwhelmed by sickness, setbacks, or detours.

But what if those circumstances are invitations to *notice*? What if by slowing down and being present, we perceive our circumstances in a whole new light? What if by noticing the good, the broken, and the future in a commingled picture, we gain clarity and understanding and hope and peace?

This is a game changer for marriage, for parenting, for being a neighbor, a friend, a colleague, a citizen of the world. A human. In fact, it's more than a game changer: this is the difference between flourishing and withering. Only when we slow down can we cultivate a habit of noticing and regard the good, the broken, and the future. So many people acknowledge this and even give lip service to the general idea of slowing down, but they can't do it. We literally feel like our life would fall apart if we altered our speed. It offends us that someone would even suggest it. We are busy. Oh, that we would slow down enough to see the beauty of our commingled story.

Presence

Mature love changes us. It builds up a longing within us to savor the moments, to be present with each breath of our lives. Our culture is moving too fast to notice much of anything. We take the good for granted. We rush past the broken. We miss the sunrise and the sunset. The sad thing is that when we miss these things, we are the ones who are diminished; we become less full. Noticing reminds us to push back against the pace of our culture and choose the mindfulness of being present in each moment with the Creator.

It's really quite shocking how much of our lives are spent mentally, emotionally, and spiritually disconnected from our physical presence. This is not without consequence! Imagine if we could conduct a "life to the full" audit in the same way we conduct an energy efficiency audit of our home. Try it. Take yourself back to a moment in your day at work, with your kids, with friends, in prayer. Imagine that you can view your life through an imaging device that captures the internal thoughts and feelings and all external dialogues and actions of your day. How much of your head and heart would be escaping from that moment in the form of distraction, control, anxiety, regret or fear? What impact might those losses have on your body, mind, relationships and spiritual health?

Something powerful takes place when we learn to be fully present physically, mentally, relationally, and spiritually. Noticing brings us into the present and demands that we move slower and engage each moment more thoughtfully and intentionally. Is it too much to suggest that worshipping created things rather than the Creator is to have an entire world of people looking down instead of looking up, fixated on small screens, shares, likes, and finger swipes? *What are we doing?* These shadows are not what we were made to see.

Can we really claim to walk in the light if we continue to notice only what we learned to see in the dark?

When we find ourselves present, and see the commingled beauty of the good, the broken, and the future, we long to embrace it, just as Jesus does. And we will. Noticing is first, then embrace. It is a progression. Just like Seeing led to Confession with Vision Up, and Surrender led to Nurture with Vision In, Noticing leads to Embracing with Vision Out. We can't skip noticing. So many of us skip right to embracing. Action! But when we do that, we don't see what it is we're meant to embrace.

Be present. Take the time to notice.

One time when my family and I visited Disney World, I asked them to slow down and take a moment to notice what was around them. We pointed out all the things we saw that were good. There were many! It was Disney World, after all. We paused a while longer to look for the broken, and there it was. In the happiest place on earth!

My kids noticed some trash on the ground that was rather out of place for the usually pristine environment. They also noticed the noise level. It was wildly loud. We noticed a young boy in a wheelchair. His limbs were twisted and his expression vacant. When my kids first noticed him, they didn't see anything broken. To them, he was just like any other person enjoying the happiest place on earth. I found their acceptance delightful. But at the same time, it allowed us to have a conversation about what it might be like when all things are made whole, when that young boy could run freely at their side. We noticed the broken commingled with the good, and we looked to the future.

My wife and I are learning to live with Vision Out each day as we help our kids develop a habit of noticing. Together we are learning to travel through our days with curiosity and wonder, looking for the good, the broken, and the future. This habit lifts our heads and opens the door to new connections, unexpected delights, honest tears, new relationships, critical thinking, and good conversation. Life to the full means noticing the commingled reality of this wonderful, complex, confusing, challenging, beautiful, tragic and exhilarating human experience.

Live slow.

Look again and again.

Look deeper.

Mature love, what do you see?

As we begin to notice what mature love sees, we find ourselves in a posture of affirming the good, acknowledging the broken, and agreeing with the future of shalom.

Seeing as Jesus sees, we are ready to embrace.

CHAPTER ELEVEN

Embracing

When we are experiencing ourselves as the beloved of God,
accepted and cherished by Him in all of our beauty and
brokenness,
our hard, rough edges start to soften.
We begin to see others as beloved as well,
and that is what gets reflected back to them
when they look into our eyes.
Not only does the love of God come to us in solitude,
the love of God begins to pour through us to others.

Ruth Haley Barton

Always the good, always the broken, always the future.

When we slow down on our trail and choose to be present, we notice that these commingled truths exist all around us. Our Vision is *out*, active, and engaged. With Perfect Love maturing within us, our heads, hearts, and hands turn outward too, ready to embrace creation.

We have become fully present, and so our love comes alive in a new way.

Embrace is shared life. Intimate life. Life together, honest and full.

If there is one word that describes the landscape of this viewpoint on our path, it is *power*: the power of genuine, holy, radical love. Love – real love, mature love, Perfect Love – is meant to be poured out. Like a rushing river flowing toward the seas, the Holy Spirit compels our heads and hearts and hands into action. Embracing means that we are free to live and act in light of what we've learned to see.

We noticed and affirmed the good, and now we embrace it in *celebration*.

We noticed and acknowledged the broken, and now we embrace it by *mourning*.

We noticed and agreed with the future, and now we embrace it by *participating*.

Embrace is both a discipline and an art. Like any other discipline or habit, we grow as we consciously practice. Although Perfect Love is transforming us from within, we still have to learn and practice a new way. The discipline of embrace involves conscious, deliberate, committed choice. It involves awareness, courage, and action. The discipline is balanced and complemented by the art. Like any other art, it requires timing, nuance, balance, and a level of wisdom and grace expressed only through communion with the Holy Spirit. Perfect Love is alive in us, teaching us both the discipline and the art.

Yes, this is a new way. And it is a way that can transform our lives and our world.

Celebrate the Good

Celebrating the good is about love expressed. True joy and gladness coming alive in relationship with others brings us to a rich and full experience of life, where love is present and alive and felt and seen. We were created to flourish in the outpouring of our delight in the good, and we were created to do it *together*.

Mature love celebrates through connection with people, even in small ways: a look, a head nod, a toast, a note, a fist bump, a smile, a wink. Celebration is present, shared, and expressed. When we celebrate the good, it changes us for the better. I have seen this happen. I have witnessed moments of intense conflict or pain where everything seems tangled and everyone seems hopeless, until one person voices something good about the situation or, one person's smile breaks the stalemate.

Celebrating the good moves us away from our own despair or discouragement about our circumstances. Of course, that doesn't mean the circumstance will change. It may be just as desperate or discouraging. What changes is our perspective, because we allow mature love to remind us that there is always something good. We know that flourishing isn't tied to circumstance, and so we are able to appreciate the good on our path, even in the midst of personal pain.

In Hawaii, "Aloha" is the language of embrace. My friend Harry Leekwai takes this to a whole new level. I haven't met anyone who more intentionally celebrates the good than Harry. If I share something with him, he genuinely delights in it, no matter what the subject matter is. His eyes light up and his ears tune in to every single word I say. He allows my joy to fill him and he returns it right back. It's astonishing because it is so rare. There is nothing small or insignificant about Harry. He celebrates people and savors moments. His joy is contagious and generative.

Many years ago, I was on a camping trip with him in the high desert of Oregon. It was late in the day and we were working hard to set up camp. Our tents were circled, and Harry was busy with the camp stoves, when all of the sudden his granddaughter ran towards him. He stopped everything he was doing, lowered his strong frame down to her level, and opened his arms wide as she ran into them. As he wrapped her in his embrace, it was clear in that moment that *she was the only thing that mattered*. His delight in her was vast and profound.

Celebrating is not for the faint of heart. It goes against everything we are taught. In this age of "terror," we are instructed to remain alert and on the lookout for anything suspicious, and this brings with it a cultural consequence. The Department of Homeland Security encourages us to report anything suspicious – "if you see something, say something", a reasonable approach to safety and security. But imagine the difference that the flip-side of this could have in our homes, our neighborhoods, cities, and nations? What if we developed a holy curiosity to find the good and celebrate it? What if our Vision Out motto became, "If you see it, celebrate it!"

Rediscovering the lost art of celebration requires margin, intention, and practice.

It could start with a simple toast at the table, with paper cups if need be. Imagine bringing friends and family together for a weekly celebration to enter the week with joy and gratitude. Taste and see the goodness of God and allow each person to express one very good thing they are grateful for. I know people who do this as a family with their teenagers at dinner. No devices, no planning logistics … just presence with one another, celebrating the goodness of the day with a shared meal prepared by everyone. What is so amazing is that these young adults *love* to be at this kind of table. We all do. In an increasingly virtual, out of touch world, we crave celebrating what is real.

This can be one of the most difficult parts of our

being to recover from the cave. We are still scarred with the old paradigm of being alone in the center; it goes deeper than we sometimes imagine. It's hard to celebrate sometimes. Bad theology, legitimate pain, depression, anxiety, fear, scarcity, and pride want to rob us of joy and celebration. We are survivalists. Our burning desire on a daily basis is to protect ourselves, but it's tough to celebrate in that posture. The lost art of celebration is recovered, little by little, toast by toast, with grins and hugs and high fives.

Life to the full does not take place in abstraction. It calls us to *real* laughter, *real* taste, *real* sight. Learning to allow the good to come close is not easy. Celebration is not implied, nor is it theoretical. It is an action – expressed, enjoyed, and shared. We were not only created and wired to enjoy experiencing good things, we were designed with the desire and the capacity to share them. Imagine the beauty of a community each adding a note to the symphony of gratitude. Celebration is an opportunity to be intentional, purposeful, and creative in our communal enjoyment of creation. This collective embrace of the good is what we were created for.

Mature love celebrates.

Mourn the Broken

Just like we intentionally make space for celebration, we

also make room for mourning. This is another deep and powerful expression of love. Mature love allows us all to wrap our arms around the broken by suffering alongside, by mourning with those who mourn and by being present. Creating space to embrace someone by suffering alongside them might be the greatest gift we can give. Just as love comes alive when we celebrate together, it also comes alive when we suffer together. No one should ever suffer alone.

Consider the Greek word, *sumpaschó*, to suffer with. This means entering the sacred place where tears fall. In that place, the call is for presence rather than problem solving. To suffer with is to honor tears, to be honest about pain, to acknowledge loss and to embrace brokenness. We do not celebrate brokenness; we embrace it. To suffer with is a costly art. Of all the arts of embrace, it may demand the most time and take the highest toll. It is uncomfortable to embrace like this, and all too often we either turn away, or we try to fix what is broken.

Over the years, I have been in many situations of suffering: hospital rooms, houses where someone has just died, front steps after a relationship has been broken, and horrific scenes of tragedy. In many of these instances, I was shocked to see just how strong my desire to "fix" was. I had to learn to honor the art of "suffering with" by laying down my impulse to fix, choosing instead to move toward, to join, and to be present with those who suffer.

One of the early lessons I learned in chaplaincy for the police department is that I had the capacity to be incredibly judgmental. I could enter a place of tears with the sole purpose, directive, and desire to suffer with those who were hurting. I possessed all the authority I needed to be present for this one job, and yet before I knew it, I found myself being critical of the way someone lived, questioning the way a person grieved, or even criticizing the way someone died. How could this be? Immature love kept me at a distance. It sanitized my behavior and became the foundation for my judgments. I quickly realized that my authority was actually an obstacle, cumbersome armor that I had to learn to put down in order to be present.

Over time I learned to put down the armor and enter into places of tears to first suffer *with* rather than bring solutions *for*. But that did not completely erase the disruption and difficulty. Places where tears are falling are hard. I have learned some practical things about the art of mourning the broken.

Physical presence matters. It matters perhaps more than anything else. By simply entering into the places where the tears fall, we allow love to enter. Appropriate touch matters, because it expresses dignity over disgust. Being there in sacred friendship physically communicates: *you are not alone, and your grief and tears are not repulsive or too much.*

Silence is okay. So often we don't have words, and so often they are not needed. As we learn to embrace, we must get comfortable with uncomfortable silence. A time of quiet presence can do far more than jumbled and confused words spoken in an effort to console.

Enter and remain. Wait. And then wait some more. Suffering with is costly because it is more than dropping by for five minutes to make an appearance. The waiting is hard, and we may feel like we aren't *doing* anything. But we are. We are present in that strange place where time is frozen and someone's world is falling apart. We are there and we remain when so many other things haven't or won't. It matters.

Pray. Commune with the Father, Son, and Spirit. The Wholly Other is there, with us and within us. We have ushered in the presence of Perfect Love. We learn to make that connection in His Presence.

Listen. There will be words, wails, worry, and confusion. We must allow ourselves to suspend searching for answers or thinking about ways to respond. Instead, we just listen to the words, the tones, the unsaid things. We allow our hearts to touch theirs, even when it brings us pain. We remain open and we listen.

Weep. We weep with those who weep. It's okay to allow our hearts to touch and our bodies to respond. Shared tears are *always* sacred tears.

Until the coming wholeness of shalom, we

cannot escape pain. It's inside *us*. It's in our families. It's in our communities, our churches, our government, our work, our children. To ignore it is to add to the brokenness. To notice it is to equalize and normalize it. To embrace it is to invite broken things towards wholeness once again, with nothing more than the presence of Perfect Love. Jesus embodied this in the most real way imaginable: God becoming human to be *with us*. Emmanuel.

I am with you. You are not alone.

This is what we need to hear when we are broken. These words change everything. They are heavenly words that communicate presence, validation, compassion, empathy, and grace. We're not fixing anything. We're simply choosing to be present in the midst of suffering. No abstraction. Choosing to mourn the broken brings us out of our own indifference. Just as celebration moves us away from despair, mourning moves us away from apathy and hopelessness. Mourning allows us to realize that our love *does* matter, that it does make a difference.

I am with you. You are not alone.

Participate in the Future

Mature love *moves*. It chooses responsibility over comfort. It remembers that it has been noticed, it has been loved and seen by the Father. And so it acts, bearing witness to the light that always follows the darkest hours of the night. Mature love moves to where things are being made new, being present in those places where it can embrace the process of mending.

Participation in the future is our movement towards shalom.

The action can be large, but honestly, it is most frequently small, simple, consistent, and hopeful. Doing the dishes, for instance. Every single time we get up from the table and we pick up plates, we shift our posture towards setting things right. This is what moves the world towards wholeness and shalom. A burden lifted, an environment restored, a trace of beauty added somewhere. A word of gossip hushed, a pattern of negativity interrupted. Speaking words of joy or peace, promoting safety or delight, recycling something, contributing to flourishing...*these are the stitches in the mending.* Everything is being set right. Everything is being made new.

The art of participation involves life at the seams. We lean in, near the fringes, where the torn places are ready for mending. We notice and identify the seams that are torn, and we look for ways to add our own stitches into the tapestry of grace. This is a life of imagination. We ask fresh questions, and we do not sit around looking for someone else to mend seams. We actively participate in setting things right by sewing reconciliation, wholeness, and shalom.

Mature love means life at the seams.

Running with Abandon

The father in the story of the prodigal son is our picture of Mature love. He runs with arms wide open, ready to embrace his son. It doesn't matter to the father whether or not he looked silly while running towards his son. It doesn't matter to the father if someone judges him for the outpouring of his love. It doesn't matter to the father that the son, *his* son, came home smelling like pigs and sweat. What mattered was love being released. What mattered was embracing his commingled son with the joy of reunion and the possibility of restoration.

That's it. That's us.

That's who we are invited to become.

Like the father, we run with abandon towards the good, the broken, and the future.

How beautiful!

We abandon any concerns about how we look in our celebration of the good. Maybe grace and mercy look foolish. Maybe forgiveness looks foolish. But mature love isn't worried about that. We aren't trying to be religiously pious or academically elite. We don't need approval or validation. Mature love is completely secure in its identity, so it can celebrate the good with abandon. We can dance and sing and rejoice and laugh.

We abandon any fear about personal loss or damage in our mourning of the broken. We aren't going to be contaminated. We aren't afraid of reputation or discomfort. The rushing river of Mature Love within us can't be tempered with such fears. Mature love overflows with grief for that which is broken, so it chooses to be near to those who weep and those who mourn. Mourning can often mean wrestling with God. Mature love knows that embracing does not mean fixing the broken things. Embracing simply means the action of joining; suffering alongside. That is enough.

We abandon any pretense of control when we choose to participate in the future. Mature love doesn't suppose it has the power to write history. Mature love simply trusts in the story that leads to redemption, wholeness, and shalom, then looks for ways to be a part of it. With imagination and vision, we speak to others about who they are and who they *will* become. Wherever there is a movement to set things right, we are there to participate.

Proximity

As we learn to embrace, we must learn to draw near. This is more than just holding someone or something closely. This is a nearness of soul and spirit, a proximity and presence that communicates Perfect Love coming alive within us. Think again of the prodigal son's father. He embraces his child, layer by layer, every part. The face of the father expresses gratitude, relief, acceptance, and joy. Proximity matters.

This is my child, the son I love, the one that I held and couldn't stop marveling at, the child that I knelt next to, watched over, and prayed for. This is the child that makes me laugh, the one that tested the limits of my love. I know his smile. I know his laughter. I know his strength. I know his weaknesses. I know what hurts him and I know what it is to be hurt by him. I love Him more than life itself.

That son.

That father.

That embrace.

Another lesson I learned as a police chaplain showed me how much nearness matters. I was tasked to provide care for a family at a nearby trailer park home. As soon as I entered the house, I immediately began to catalog offenses: dogs, garbage, food, clutter, disrepair, smell. It was revolting. The filth and stench were so overwhelming that it made my stomach turn. I found myself immediately judging the people and the situation. Part of me wanted to leave, and fast.

And yet, I was there, intentionally present with the reality of our commingled existence. I remember making a choice that day towards mature love instead of what my personal disgust reaction was triggering in me. So... *I sat down*. Right in the mess. I sat on a chair. And I *listened.*

I could have raced through my checklist which would have gotten me out of there fast: choose a funeral home, pass on family support resources, list next steps to help the grieving process. But I realized that what *they* needed in that moment was dignity. Their pain needed to be witnessed and embraced. My nearness, my choice to sit in the mess and be present, was the foundation of shalom.

The nearness, the proximity of embrace communicates dignity, compassion, and love. Proximity requires wisdom. Mature love is wise. It recognizes the moment for embrace, but it also recognizes when an embrace could do harm. When embrace is not possible, mature love waits and prays. Mature love always hopes. It knows that one day every wound will close. Every war will cease. There will be no more violence and no more injustice. Until that day, it hopes and believes that embrace is possible. Mature love remains open, waiting and praying for the moment it can run out to embrace the other.

Courage

Love matures until there is no fear in embrace.

There are proper times for waiting, but many times our habits, biases, and fears hold us back from embracing the good, the broken, and the future. This is the space and time when our movement toward shalom slows or comes to a stop. I know it when I see it, because I have done it. I have allowed fear to creep in and rob my courage, constricting and chilling my heart until I turned away.

First, fear succeeds when we are afraid to embrace the good. To embrace the good is to become vulnerable to loss. If we taste joy ... we might lose it. If we find love ... it might be taken away. We cling tightly to what we *think* we possess. We are too afraid to let go so that we can embrace all the good around us.

Second, fear succeeds when we spurn the broken. Humans have a disgust reaction that prevents us from smelling, tasting, or touching things that our brain has judged to be "unclean."[57] Studies indicate that once our brains file something or someone away as unclean or disgusting, it is almost impossible to overcome that disgust reaction. Designed to keep us from becoming ill, endangered, contaminated, or dirty, our disgust reaction demands that we *reject* the embrace of anything we have deemed unclean. We succumb to this. We give in to fear. We refuse to embrace the broken.

Lastly, fear succeeds when we are afraid to embrace the future. We fear the future because we can't precisely determine it or control it. Our need to know and control robs us of the joy of anticipation and the purpose of participation. We are risk averse, so we choose to sit out. Fear of disappointment holds us hostage from working for the future we hope for. We lack certainty, so we hold our cards and play it safe.

Perfect Love, alive in us, matures until there is no room for doubt and fear.

"Such love has no fear, because perfect love expels all fear."[58]

Given this context, it is easy to see why Jesus' way was so strange and disruptive. He was a master of embrace, so much so that some suggested that He was a "glutton and a drunkard, and a friend of tax collectors and other sinners!"[59] He loved creation, and He took time to break bread, to eat fish, and to enjoy friends. He embraced brokenness in every form, touching diseased skin, welcoming outcasts, and embracing those labeled unclean. He embraced the future in the most tangible, powerful, sacrificial way possible, giving His life itself to participate in the coming shalom. His light drove out darkness. His love drove out fear. He welcomed a new age where love conquers fear over and over again in a million moments of embrace.

This Jesus is *alive within us*, remember?

This love is the same love that conquers our own fears.

As His life and love mature in us, we learn to see the good, the broken and the future commingled in us and around us with every step. His love calls us to the front lines, past the edge of our fears. Christ in us will slow us down, press us beyond our disgust, past our timidity, and through our risk aversion. He invites us to embrace beauty that we would otherwise rush past, brokenness that without Him would cause us to recoil, and a future wholeness that we can participate in with our heads, our hearts, and our hands.

This is life to the full.

The full measure of gratitude, of compassion, of hope. The full measure of love.

And now, we are ready to be poured out.

CHAPTER TWELVE

Love

Love isn't something we fall into;
love is someone we become.

Bob Goff

The end of the matter is love.

The flattened ceiling is lifted, and the fiction is made new. Fear is defeated. Our outward response floods our entire experience of life with the one thing that remains: love. Love pours over and into the commingled channels of the good and the broken and the future like the rushing river breaking through the dam. This is life to the full. This is the end of all things and the beginning of all things.

Life to the full has led us to something we didn't quite expect: a poured-out life.

We are spent, poured out in celebration, in mourning, and in participation with the future. It is a new sort of "spent"; not the exhaustion of restlessness, not the weariness of numbing, but the satisfying realization that Christ in us has *animated us*, and that our love matters just as His love matters. This is a good spent, like the endorphin-saturated feeling of a race well run. It is the exhale of life to the full.

From this place we turn back to the source once again. Jesus. The loop of our trail comes full circle. Our love has been poured out *from* the source back *to* the source. In turning back to Him, we are filled up again and again. It's the loop. The more we look to Him, the more we look like Him. The more we look like Him, the more we look with Him. And the more we look with Him, the more we look back up and see Jesus, the source of human flourishing.

The Vision is Jesus.

The Poured-Out Life

The scriptures tell the story of a woman who came to pour her love out for Jesus.[60] Just a few days before His death, she brought the most expensive thing she owned: an alabaster jar of perfume. She broke the jar in His presence, inviting the scorn of all who witnessed, and proceeded to anoint Him with the precious oil.

Imagine Jesus, about to have his own body shattered and His life poured out. What must He have felt, seeing this woman smashing her life's savings to allow the treasure inside to spill out and pour over Him?

Surely, He noticed the beauty of her sacrifice, the good of it, a significance that she herself could not have seen. He probably observed the recoiling gasps of those who couldn't understand this sort of extravagance. And He must have agreed with the future, knowing the redemption to come. I imagine pain searing through His heart while at the same moment a smile lighting up His face. His embrace of her outpouring is recorded in multiple accounts. Though it confounded those who witnessed it, Jesus must have been filled with gratitude, compassion, and hope.

A few days later, He hung on a cross, His arms outstretched. Defenseless, broken, blood flowing out. As His consciousness began to fade, I imagine Jesus drifting back to the image of the woman smashing her jar, the contents spilling out, the anointing. What prayer might He have prayed in His moments of surrender?

Father, may it be. Shatter this jar of clay and pour out this life for theirs. Empty me so that they might have life to the full.

This is the story of love. Aged, precious, mature, poured out, and spilling over.

We found this love when we looked up. We found this love maturing inside of us when we looked in. And this is the love we find in the moments when we stretch our own arms out and look out.

Love pours out in celebration, and life and

beauty appear.

Love pours out in mourning, and life and beauty appear.

Love pours out in mending at the seams, and life and beauty appear.

The reality of Perfect Love within us is that *we were never meant to store it up*. It was meant to mature, to spill over and pour out until there is nothing left. The final movement of love is always to be given away. And the ongoing movement of the Creator is to restore. He is the source of this love, the source that never runs dry.

There are so many who get, but don't have it.

What does it mean to have it?

To have it is to release love. To be poured out. The love that has been birthed and nurtured within us leads us out with new vision.

The Vision is Jesus.

Look to Him. Look like Him. Look with Him.

This is life to the full.

Love Embodied

Each day, we become more and more like Jesus. As we learn to embrace, others begin to see and experience the reality of Jesus as *His* love pours out through us. He is embracing *us*, bringing us back into communion with Himself, refueling and restoring all that is spent. Our own desires and needs lessen as we allow Christ to give

Himself from within us. Our physical, tangible, human form begins to embody the love of the Father.

Our celebration becomes selfless when we choose to rejoice over others. When we see others succeeding, learning, and growing, we have no sense of comparison or competition, just love. We can step aside and marvel at the goodness in others, joy spilling over as the Father's delight for His children comes alive in us. When we can spend our time and our energy in celebration of another rather than in preference of ourselves, we have experienced mature love.

Our mourning becomes selfless when we surrender any desires to fix or control, or any agenda whatsoever. We show up simply to be poured into the wounds. We feel no need to recoil or fear or turn away. We are selfless in our presence, embracing in the places where the tears fall. We give of ourselves to the lonely, to the weak, to the vulnerable, to the grieving. When we can count it an honor to pour ourselves out in this way, we have experienced mature love.

Our participation becomes selfless when we say yes to setting things right. We don't walk away from the present without adding a stitch to mend the future, even when it costs us deeply. The space for the stranger. The food for the hungry. The voice for the voiceless. These moments are present and waiting, and all of creation is groaning for us to say yes to them. When we choose the kind word, the gentle way, the powerful protest, the hopeful song, at the expense of our own comfort and convenience, we have experienced mature love. We allow ourselves to be *completely spent* in the effort to participate in the coming shalom.

We live a life of love, because that's all that remains. Celebration flows from us as we embrace the good, and this births *gratitude*. Mourning flows from us as we embrace the broken, and this births *compassion*. Participation in setting things right and making things whole flows from us as we embrace the future, and this births *hope*. Love pours into these three channels and all of it travels back to the source so that it can be poured out once again.

Gratitude. Compassion. Hope. The heart postures of a poured-out life.

Gratitude

Embracing the good in celebration ultimately cultivates gratitude. We find true beauty, true goodness, and true flourishing. We can do nothing less than overflow in gratitude and thanksgiving to the Creator. Here, in the middle of our mess, our brokenness, our sin and shame and humanity, He allows good. He celebrates good. He creates good. We are grateful. We are thankful.

Our eyes turn back up. Like the water that evaporates from the rivers and oceans, we look back up to the source. As we celebrate strangers and neighbors, families and towns, habitats and the beauty of the Earth, we look to the source. We celebrate that which is good. We experience gratitude. It is the song on our lips and the posture of our hearts.

This gratitude does not happen in abstraction. This is not about thank you notes or obligatory acknowledgements, although those are good. This is not something forced or planned. This is the overflow. This is as good as it gets, life to the full, brimming over and breaking the dam and tangibly expressing thanksgiving for every good thing.

The life and beauty we longed for in the cave is alive in front of us, alive so deeply and fully and powerfully that it fills our hearts with overflowing joy. It seems more real, more stunning, more holy, more transformational than ever before. Relational not circumstantial. The sound of a bird singing at dawn. The perfection of a cool breeze on a warm day. The expression of kindness on the face of a child. The connections in relationship with friends new and old. Our gratitude moves our hearts beyond what we thought we had the capacity to feel. Songs and prayers and tears and laughter well up in us because our human bodies are not capable of containing this sort of thanksgiving for that which is good.

Compassion

From thin fractures of the heart to the chasms of devastated cities, mature love sees hurt and fear and regret. It sees racism, injustice, violence and abuse. Mature love recognizes lust, greed, deceit, and pride. It sees the lonely and the outcast, the refugee and the bullied. It sees those who mourn and those who feel betrayed. Mature love witnesses disease and pollution. It sees giving up and giving in. It sees the reasons that we don't speak. It sees the pain that we try to hide. Mature love recognizes failure and suffering and decay and death. All of it.

The response of mature love to these things? It is not fear or hopelessness.

It is not shame or despair or regret or anger.

It is not indifference.

The response is compassion.

Compassion is disruption deep inside us that moves us to suffer *with* another. It is a feeling so strong that it compels us to draw near enough to embrace the broken. Scripture uses this kind of language to describe God being close enough to touch us. "The Lord is close to the brokenhearted."[61]

Compassion does not take place in abstraction. Sympathetic emojis decorating our text threads do not express the gut-wrenching, bowel-unsettling force of compassion that Jesus demonstrated. When He saw a widow weeping as the body of her only son was carried out through a city gate, he was moved with immense compassion. "He walked over to the coffin and touched it,"[62] coming near enough to touch both the shattered life and the broken heart.

What an incredible honor to draw near, to bear witness, and to share in suffering and tears. Do we think about it this way? We should. In these holy moments, when compassion flows, the love of the Father flows through us to His children. These are the moments of deep communion between Creator and creatures. This humbles us and reminds us to be slow to speak and quick to listen. Our presence and compassion in the midst of suffering ushers in the presence and compassion of Christ.

In these moments we confess, "We do not know what to do, but we are looking to you for help."[63] Have mercy, Lord, in these situations where we don't have the capacity to understand or fix. Compassion allows us to love in a way that we otherwise cannot. It allows us to enjoy the company of those who seldom enjoy company, to see the forgotten and remind them of their inherent worth, to recognize the anguish that no one else notices, and to be present in places of tears. Compassion flows from our embrace and gives purpose to our noticing of the broken.

When we choose compassion for the broken

one, we foster compassion for *all*. At all times, in all seasons, the posture of our heart towards humanity remains compassionate. We have seen God in a new way, we have seen ourselves in a new way, and now we see others in a new way... with our Father's eyes of compassion and love.

Hope

Mature love experiences hope that is deep and abiding, rooted in relationship to the One who is making all things new. The seams and scars of reconciliation are signs of shalom and evidence of a beauty unlike anything else in the whole world. The stitching together of what has been torn apart holds the DNA of a new creation. Whether fabric or skin or story or reality, the seams where pieces have been torn apart and mended again are the beacons of wholeness.

Jesus Himself invited Thomas and His other disciples to see and feel the holes in His hands and feet. The scars in the physical body of Jesus revealed the seam where our relationship with God was reconciled, the highest display of love evidenced, right at the seam. Grace. Forgiveness. Life and beauty. Our lives woven into His. Our scars hidden in His. Our flourishing threaded into relationship with the One we were made by and for.

Recognizing these threads means seeing the future in the small things and participating in it with passionate hope. Mature love does not despise small beginnings; it joins, one thread and one stitch at a time. This is how peace shows up in the most unlikely places. Shalom appears in the *little by little*.

While there continue to be wars and rumors of wars, while refugees continue to be ripped from their homes, can you see the threads? While city after city across the globe is sent reeling in the wake of senseless violence, and America continues on a fractured trajectory, can you see the threads? We will not find them in headlines, broadcasts, or social media campaigns. They are smaller. They invite us to look closer. They are in our own neighborhoods, in our churches and families, and in the fabric of our own hearts.

My youngest daughter loves to make jewelry. She will carefully string beads together through tiny pieces of colored thread. When she is done, she asks me to help her tie the loose ends together. Simple … but not easy. Every time I try to do it, it feels like I am wearing a pair of cheap, puffy, insulated snow gloves, three sizes too big and impossible to work with. If I don't give careful time and attention to the tying of one thread, all the beads fall off. Tying the small threads is the big work of reconciliation.

Participating in the future means *not only recognizing those threads but operating with the hope that they matter*. This hope believes that what has been torn can be mended by giving careful attention to single threads. Shalom is pioneered through humble conversation, honest confession, heartfelt repentance, loving mercy, and gracious forgiveness. Peace is sought for and birthed in individual, quiet meals rather than spectacular ordeals. Wholeness is achieved by seeing torn things made new rather than discarded.

Just like gratitude and compassion, our hope does not happen in abstraction. There are no neutral words. There are no insignificant thoughts, emotions, or actions. They all *participate in* or *work against* the "webbing together of God, humans, and all creation in justice, fulfillment and delight."[64] This is the weight of mature love.

Every thread matters.

Hope gives us the boldness to act. Hope invites us to engage and pour out our energies for the glory of God and the benefit of others, to spend and be spent for that which participates in and contributes to shalom. Makoto Fujimura uses the term, "boarder-stalkers," for those who live near the seams, near the edge, seeing with imagination and empathy.[65] We believe there is nothing that cannot be made new.

Our prayer becomes, "May your Kingdom come soon. May your will be done on earth, as it is in heaven."[66] We surrender the outcome of our outpouring and we trust His timing and provision. Our hope is not in our ability to participate well with His future, but rather simply in His promise of the dawn. Our effort is not to bring about the new age of shalom, but to traverse to the seams, watching and waiting with hope for it to come.

Anywhere something is being set right, Jesus is there. He is ahead of us, and behind us, and with us, and within us. He's uniting with us at the dawn of that new age. This is His kingdom and it's coming. This is the right side of history. This is where the thread that *we* are stitching meets the thread that *He* is stitching. We find ourselves face-to-face with the One who's ushering in the new day, the author of shalom itself.

Anchored by hope, mature love sees the future, a future where oppression is lifted, where there is mature love between neighbors. It sees families reconciled and friendships restored. This future sees justice and equality and the end of all war and conflict. It sees disease healed and earth honored. It sees hearts opening and wounds closing. It sees prodigals returning home. Mature love sees clear rivers and quiet forests. It sees the timid leading and the mighty empowering them to see anew. It sees no more tears, no more death, no more sadness. It sees a simple seed of justice producing peace for thousands. It sees new songs and new beauty. It sees every tribe and nation sharing joy.

Freedom

Mature love is a love that thrives in the wide, open spaces of freedom. As gratitude, compassion, and hope become the postures of our hearts, we discover that we are free to experience life to the full. We are free to pursue joy, fulfillment, delight, and relationship. And yet, we long to do what is best for God and for others. In fact, we long to *prefer* God and others. So, what shall we do with this freedom?

The scriptures tell us that all things are permissible, but not all things are beneficial.[67] Mature love learns to understand the balance between possibility and limit. Mature love prefers another, choosing to limit its freedom to what is beneficial for those it loves. If I desire a certain thing, but it makes my wife uncomfortable or costs my children something precious, then I will limit that possibility out of love. I will choose away from my desire, not because I am captive but because I am free.

We see this in creation. Sunrise opens the door to possibility, and sunset brings the retreat of the light. We witness creation itself recognizing and honoring its limits, it's design to rest. Ordered in a perfect balance of possibility and limit, we witness an elaborate, magnificently choreographed dance of mutual submission. Evening and morning. Light and dark. Crashing tide and surrendered coastline. In this delicate balance of power, it is possible for incredibly vulnerable, seemingly powerless forms of life and beauty to enjoy fellowship and even communion. But when this balance is disrupted or violated, unspeakable harm comes, usually to the most vulnerable.

Mature love holds this tension in balance, experiencing life to the full while selflessly preferring others.

Jennifer's Garden

Jennifer was beautiful. A young mom in her late 30's, she and her husband had two young boys and a seemingly flourishing life. But all was not as it seemed. Jennifer concealed a private struggle with depression. Even those closest to her had no idea the pain and brokenness she carried inside.

One night she went missing. Her husband reached out to a police officer who attended our church. A search party formed, and our little church embraced and cared for the group that looked for her. Days turned into weeks before the tragic news shattered her family and our small town.

Jennifer had taken her own life.

In the midst of that tragedy, new relationships were formed. My life became fused together with Jennifer's parents, her husband, and her kids. I remember the hours spent crying on the front steps of our old, stone church, hurting for this family who had lost one they held so dear.

In the year following Jennifer's death, I would often make time to join her family, to listen, and to embrace. One Christmas Eve, I brought our kids with me to visit Jennifer's mom. We brought a bouquet of red flowers and some hearts full of love. We talked for a bit before I began to notice some leaves which had collected in the yard. I saw a simple thread and offered a hand to rake her yard and remove the leaves.

As I left that day, my mind drifted into the future. I remembered a conversation that I had had with a hospital chaplain once. He talked about the deep fear of being forgotten or forgetting loved ones who had died, especially for children. As I remembered this, I glimpsed an opportunity to come right up against the seam dividing the seen and unseen, to somehow affirm the reality that those we lose are more present than we may realize. I wanted Jennifer's boys to remember her, and for her life and beauty to be part of their memory. I knew we needed to create space for that remembrance to come alive.

At the time our church operated a beautiful home called the Hillside Inn, a place for prodigals to find a space to rest, heal, and grow. The Inn sat on a large corner lot on the very edge of a small town in Oregon, right where the sidewalk disappears into the Red Hills of wine country. It was a beautiful space, but the yard had not been cultivated. Another thread began to take form in my mind and heart.

What if, in this place, at this commingled intersection of good and broken and future, we honored Jennifer's story? What if we created a garden that Jennifer's boys could enter and remember their mom? What if that place could offer hope, even in the midst of great tragedy? What if this garden was open and yet set apart, free for the weary and thirsty, the heavy laden, the broken, those privately carrying the great pain of depression? What if they could find rest?

Jennifer's Garden was born from this thread. Time was given, treasure was laid, little by little until an entire community gathered in embrace. That very good ground was touched by hands animated by the Spirit of Perfect Love. Jennifer's family joined the creative work, adding subtle and intentional remembrances that would have been special and pleasing to their beloved.

Her story, her life, and her death were not hidden. There was no sense of shame or disgrace, only the honesty of real loss, real mourning, and a place to be near the hurting and the broken. The good, broken, and future commingled here in this place, embraced by Perfect Love. Wounds found healing with every load of bark and every plant nurtured. It was absolutely stunning to see the dawn of so much light flood right into the darkness. Gratitude, compassion, and hope echoed through the hearts of all who came to the garden.

Love was *alive*.

The Father

When I picture the father of the prodigal son resting in the cool of the morning, I try to imagine who and what he saw as he looked out at creation. What must have been in his head and heart on the day that his son came home? Seasoned with gratitude, tempered by compassion, and anchored in hope. He was living life at the seams, watching and waiting for a moment not yet seen but fully believed. Perhaps he paused that morning, noticing the beauty of the new day. The power of creation revealing the mutual submission of creatures. A moment of peace in the midst of disruption. A prayer of faith offered with hope.

At mid-day, tired and thirsty, he looks out and recognizes the substance of things hoped for appearing on the horizon. His son! His son is coming home! He leaves everything and begins to run. By now his faith is becoming sight, and within moments he feels the weight of his son collapse into his arms.

The first thing he sees is the beauty of his young son. He sees his eyes and the way his head turns when he smiles. Beautiful. Oh, the *gratitude* he must feel in this moment. Their shoulders touch and heads press together.

There is no recoiling, no retreating. He feels the tears on the face of his son, and without hearing a word recognizes how deeply broken he is. Oh, the *compassion* that overflows in light of the brokenness. Scorched by the sun and weary from the walk, the son grasps his father as the father embraces even more. Together they rest. There is *hope* here. Father holding son. Full heir. Fully restored. Fully embraced and loved.

The father begins, in real and powerful ways, to walk with his son into the future. He communicates with every act that here, at home, he can find rest. He is forgiven. He is loved. The father is already imagining the joy that is coming. He sees the celebration. An evening already unfolding with dancing, feasting, neighbors, friends, and a family made whole.

May we live a life of love, poured out to overflow. Just as the father who embraced his prodigal son. Just as the community who rallied around a broken family and planted a garden. Just as the woman who shattered everything that was precious to her in an expression of radical love for Jesus. Just as Christ Himself, who stretched His arms wide on a cross and broke Himself open to overflow.

I invite you to imagine yourself standing with arms outstretched, looking up. The image of the cross, the image of Jesus, the image of Perfect Love. May this image be upon you and within you.

The Vision is Jesus.

Look to Him. Look like Him. Look with Him.

This is life to the full.

EPILOGUE

Spirit of the living God,
come fall afresh on me.
Come wake me from my sleep.
Blow through the caverns of my soul.
Pour in me to overflow.

Jeremy Riddle

Our trail continues in a loop, covering more and more ground as we experience life to the full. We walk this road until we see Love face to face. We experience more and more flourishing as life and beauty continue to appear. Each time we return to a scenic viewpoint along the trail, we discover more depth, more beauty, more life.

We have been recalibrated and have rediscovered our identity as creatures. We are not alone, and we are not in the center. Comfortable in this identity we confess that are we uniquely made with value, purpose, and dignity. We look up. We look in. And we look out. Love has come alive in us, and fear has died. We embrace the creation, embodying the Perfect Love of our Creator, overflowing with gratitude, compassion, and hope.

Life to the full is living in the balance and flow of adoration, transformation, and love.

The Landscape

It would not serve you well to leave you with this trail guide and not make some sort of commentary on the landscape you must traverse. The map you see in this book shows a high-altitude view of hills and valleys, towns and countrysides, forests and meadows. The terrain we travel in this life is similar, but at ground level we are highly aware of the rocky paths, the switchbacks, the rapids, and the darkness.

In short: *there is peril ahead.*

This peril exists, not because of the path we have chosen, but because the landscape itself is broken. Shalom has been violated in our stories and on our planet but also in the entirety of our existence. We believe in a coming wholeness. This is why we choose to travel at the seams, because all is not mended yet. Darkness has been defeated but has not yet been destroyed. It pursues us outside the cave, *especially* outside the cave. Choosing the path of life to the full does not transform the landscape; it transforms us.

We will experience trauma, suffering, loss, pain, and death. When we find ourselves facing a summit that seems insurmountable, or we find ourselves in a forest so dark and dense that we will surely lose our way, or we find our backs against a wall and our faces scorched by the sun, we will hear the luring voice of the counter-whisper tempting us to return to the safety of the cave. We will feel the sting of evil as it grasps at us from the shadows. If we wander off the trail, or look to our right or our left, the cave mouth is there and ready to swallow us whole. While we walk this loop of life to the full, the haunting sound of the cave will sometimes crescendo to a full-fledged roar. The counter-whisper that it manufactures will sound like truth in the moments when we are weakened and weary.

There is peril ahead.

But our sight has changed. We see the peril, but that is not *all* we see. We see that the mountain that slowed us down allowed us to forge the strength we needed. We see that the forest where we got lost allowed us to discover something beautiful in its depths. We see the future wholeness of the terrain as it will be. We experience healing of scorched faces and wounded limbs, of broken hearts and silenced fears. We see that the road signs pointing us back to the cave only exist to destroy our freedom and our flourishing, and we courageously press onward towards dawn. Now we see.

Our vision is Jesus. We will not forget the moment our chains were broken by the Perfect Love that came into the cave and paid for our freedom. Although the danger is real, we recognize that the haunting sound of the cave is a LIE. The cave has been overcome. It was not and is not reality. The commingled path we now travel is reality. We come to see that the existence and persistence of the danger of the cave now only serves to prove that we are on the path of truth, and flourishing, and life to the full.

Beg to Differ

Is your desire to see balance restored and creation flourish? Do you long to see life and beauty where there has been harm and devastation? We have not achieved balance yet. Our arms strain to grasp it, but we are not quite strong enough, and we cannot reach quite far enough. It's like trying to hold oil in our hands; when we capture a bit, the rest slips through. At our best we continue to look forward into the future, imagining how we might try again. But we will grow weary and exhausted.

This is why the incarnation represents the miracle of all miracles. For in it and through it, we see an arm stronger than ours. The Creator himself enters to break this cycle. He addresses the deepest violations and the deepest injuries to restore peace to every area of conflict. Every violation between Creator and creature, every conflict within us and conflict that exists between us, even our struggle with creation itself. In Christ we see the Creator making total peace possible in every area of disruption.

A first century philosopher once said, "Light says to the darkness, 'I beg to differ.'"[68]

What can lay claim to darkness like light? Being in love and in life with Jesus. Love says to a flattened age, "We beg to differ." These are revolutionary words.

We beg to differ.

We will not be deceived by the counter-whisper that calls us back to the cave.

We will not fade into the darkness.

The Vision is Jesus. He continues to speak. His presence still enters the darkness and His Voice always asks, "Do you believe?"

Three words become our daily confession, the confession behind a life of adoration, transformation, and love. *Now I See.* These are enchanted words spoken, from the dust outside the cave. These were Celidonius' words. Oh, now I see. *I see!* These are the words of captives set free and prodigals who come home, humbled and alive!

May we be pioneers of a new age, young and old, crossing every racial, socio-economic, political, and cultural divide to form one body with one vision. May we be a new generation of witnesses who with our lips and our lives boldly proclaim, *I was blind, but Now I See.* May the semblances of life and beauty overwhelm our senses and our souls. May the invitation to truly see resonate so deeply within us that we run out of the cave into the wide, open spaces of freedom. May the life that we experience overflow and pour out into those around us. May they see the Truth of Jesus alive in our outstretched arms. May we become love as we watch and wait for the dawn.

VU VI VO

The Vision Is Jesus.

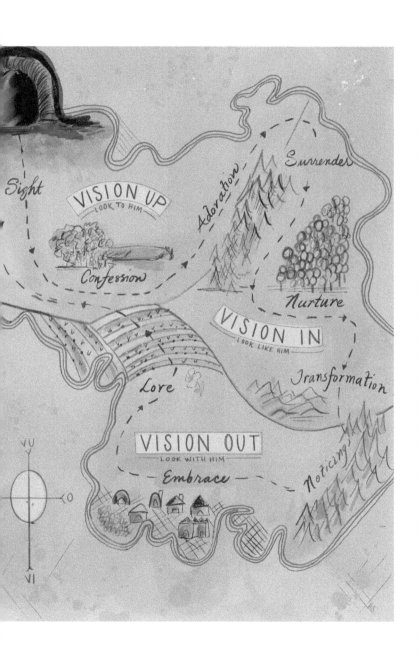

AFTERWORD

I pray that you hear the invitation.
I pray that you listen, search, and find the One who calls.
I pray you do not do this alone.

I pray you find a community of people who desire to look to Him, look like Him, and look with Him. The richest part of this experience is sharing life to the full together. The church is not a place, it is a people. An adoring, transforming, and radically loving people whose lips and lives confess: *we were blind, but now we see.*

And I would love to hear from you! I would love to hear your stories and share in the good, the broken, and the future. The journey is always more beautiful together.

You can share your stories of life to the full at www.zachjelliott.com.

ACKNOWLEDGEMENTS

From Zach:

This book would not exist without the very real love and faithfulness of God. My gratitude for this opportunity, the partners I have the honor of recognizing, and the work itself begins and ends at the Source.

There is no way to retrace every step and acknowledge every person who has contributed to this work. In some way each page contains your influence. Every relationship, each conversation, the shared books, and all the experiences that we have enjoyed are a part of this story. If our paths have crossed, even for a moment, I want to thank you for your contribution to this work and to this story.

To Cammie: Thank you for your constant love, encouragement, and sacrifice. Your strength and bravery are matched only by the selflessness and inner beauty that we all witness each day. You have provided wise and steady counsel at each important step, with powerful support at precisely the right time. You have moved mountains in order to see this work complete. Adoration, transformation, and love are your way. Thank you for making these truths visible. The fullness of your life pours into our family and changes our world. My admiration for you deepens daily, and I cherish every moment with you. Now let's eat cake!

To Bella, Holland, Olivia, and Jude: Thank you for leaning into this adventure. You have been so patient and such an incredible team throughout the process. I love you so much and I am deeply grateful for your prayers, notes, encouraging words, and all the fun celebrations along the way. Thank you for believing in me and for walking the trail with mom and I. Us Together. We did it! Here's to less screen time!

To my friend and coach Jay Puppo: There is no way to adequately thank you for your investment in my life and in our project. Your influence has deepened and enriched my life, my marriage, and my ministry. Thank you for walking this journey out each week and for keeping me accountable to stay in the submarine. Here is to our beautiful someday goals and each domino in between!

To my incredible friend and co-writer Rebecca Sandberg: Thank you for bringing this story to life and making it truly beautiful. Your wisdom, creativity, and unwavering commitment to finish this work well brought fresh inspiration at every turn. I marvel at your capacity to exercise your gift with words with such sensitivity to the Spirit and to the book. Here's to all the drafts, the thousands of emails, hours of calls, and your Jedi ability to interpret my hand signals, arm waving, and "rattling" audio recordings from 3000 miles away. You are a marvelous writer and a true friend. It is the joy of a lifetime to share life and beauty with your family. You have forever changed our lives.

To Lost Poet Press: Thank you for your commitment to communicating "truth and hope to hearts that are searching for it." You have done that for me, and I am honored to now share in that work together. I am deeply grateful that you chose to "give a voice and a platform" to Now I See. It was a joy to entrust this project to you.

To my friend, publisher and partner in the gospel, Melody Farrell: There are no coincidences. I am brought low by the strange, powerful, and incredibly precise ways that God accomplishes His purposes. When I look back at the layers to the story that needed to be true in order to bring this project into your care, I am speechless. Only God could have carried it across the country to place it in the hands of someone with such creative capacity, theological integrity, and pastoral insight. Your work on this book is far deeper than that of a publisher. Your care for the message and the messengers is a gift that I treasure. Thank you for saying yes, for shepherding these words, and for making it possible for us to share them with the world.

To Jerome and Erin Milner: Very rarely will someone leave everything and move across the country to a city completely foreign to them. Even more rare are those who would leave everything to share in a journey with friends and see to it that a work is finished. You have done this and so much more with humility and grace. Your faith and selflessness have taught me so much about mature love. Thank you for pouring out your lives in partnership for the gospel. Here's to life, beauty, and the adventure ahead.

To my friend and partner in the gospel, Fr. Sean Flannery: Thank you for sharing books, dreams, and struggles together. Your partnership made me a better pastor and I am a better person because of our friendship. Your influence continues to shape my imagination and encourage me into the wild. Here is to more NF'ery!

To the V3 support network: Us Together. Those words hang on our wall, but they echo in our hearts and steel our minds each step of the way. Your years of constant prayer and radical love have left a mark on our hearts and the hearts of so many. I cannot thank you enough for your partnership in the gospel and for your care of our families. Thank you for helping us to share the gospel + love the church. This project is just one example, one part of the larger story that you are helping to write. Here's to the things that we have yet to ask or imagine. We love you.

My life and this book owe a great debt to the cloud of witnesses who have penned words that have stirred my faith, inspired my imagination, and shaped my thinking. This book echoes with thoughts influenced by Francis Schaeffer and John Muir, St. Augustine and Charles Taylor, Bonhoeffer and Lewis, Rudolph Otto and Lossky, Montfort and Hildebrand, Ellen Charry and G.K. Beale, Peterson and Plantinga, Luther and Norwich, Heschel and so many others. My gratitude for the hearts of the poets, scholars, theologians, and wordsmiths is beyond measure.

From Rebecca:

This entire endeavor has been a journey of faith, a journey that for me would not be possible without the intense love of Jesus who pursues us when we are lost. I am ever grateful and humbled by the love of Jesus. I look to Him and I love Him.

Thank you, Zach and Cammie. Your friendship is rare and beautiful. I am forever changed by your commingled view of people and your love of Jesus. Your sacrifice and love for our family continues to amaze me. I am astonished by the depth and level of friendship that we share. So much life and beauty! It is unlike anything I have never known. Zach, thank you for asking me to participate in this incredible work. It has been the gift of lifetime! Thank you for trusting me to come alongside this project in real time and in real life and for your patience as I wrestled and questioned so much. You can still send audio recordings!

Thank you, Melody, my new friend at Lost Poet Press. I am so glad that we got to work together on this project. You are amazing at what you do. I will miss our Wednesday morning check-ins. This could have not been done without you!

Thank you, dear friends Kathleen, Nora and Sara. I love doing life in community with each one of you in the good and the broken. Your authenticity and willingness to show up is fertile soil for love to grow. I am in awe of what true friendship does for the world…little by little…one day at a time. Kathleen, thank you, thank you, thank you for leaning in and reading manuscripts and giving honest and beautiful feedback.

Thank you, kind husband, Roger. God is faithful and good. Thank you for your love and support in this project and in life. Thanks for reading paragraphs and chapters and manuscripts and giving feedback. Thank you for your prayers. I felt them. It is a rare gift to know and be known. Thank you for being my friend on this wild journey of transformation, growth and love. Every day is a gift and a new day.

Thank you, to my young adult people-children, Jake, Andrew and Maggie. The vision is Jesus. You three are hilarious and fun, thoughtful and kind. So incredibly grateful for each one of you. Thank you for your encouragement as I typed and typed. Thank you for being willing to learn with me and embody the message of this book.

Thank you, Newberg, for the life and beauty of a small town.

Thank you ice cream socials, potlucks, picnics, gatherings and feasts for providing space for life and beauty to grow!

REFERENCES

Foreword
Isaiah 43:19 NLT

Prologue
Eldredge, John. *Waking the Dead: The Glory of a Heart Fully Alive*. Thomas Nelson, 2003, p. 1.

Chapter 1
Tolkien, J.R.R. *The Hobbit*. Revised Edition, Random House, 1982, p. 75.

Chapter 2
Lewis, C.S. *Mere Christianity*. Harper One, 2015, pp. 136-137.

Chapter 3
Mumford and Sons. "Awake My Soul". *Sigh No More*, Island Records, 2009.

Chapter 4
Manning, Brennan. *The Ragamuffin Gospel*. First Hardcover Edition, Multnomah, 2005, p. 90.

Chapter 5
Muir, John. *John of the Mountains, The Unpublished Journals of John Muir.* Compiled by Linnie Marsh Wolfe. The University of Wisconsin Press, Houghton Mifflin Edition reprinting, 1966, pp. 191-192.

Chapter 6
Heber, Reginald. "Thrice Holy". *The World's Great Religious Poetry*, edited by Caroline Miles Hill, Ph.D., The Macmillian Company, 1942, p. 529.

Chapter 7

Augustine. *The Confessions of St. Augustine*. Translated by Rex Warner, Signet, A Mentor Book, 1963, p. 20.

Chapter 8
Lennon, John. "Man of the Decade Interview". Filmed at Ascot, Berkshire, ATV, 2nd December 1969, D.M. Beatles site, https://www.dmbeatles.com/interviews.php?interview=69 .

Chapter 9
1 John 3:2 NLT

Chapter 10
Rohr, Richard. *Everything Belongs*. Revised and Updated Edition, Crossroad Publishing, 2003, p. 56.

Chapter 11
Barton, Ruth Haley. *Invitation to Solitude and Silence*. Expanded Second Hardcover Edition, InterVarsity Press, 2010, p. 133.

Chapter 12
Goff, Bob. *Everybody Always*. Nelson Books, 2018, p. 2.

Epilogue
Jeremy Riddle. "Fall Afresh". *Furious*, Mercy/Vineyard Publishing, 2011.

---

[1] Paraphrase of John 10:10

[2] Influenced by the work of Cornelius Plantinga, Jr. *Not the Way it's Supposed to Be: A Breviary of Sin*. Eerdmans Pub. Co., 1995, p. 10.

[3] Paraphrase of Proverbs 29:18

[4] Greig, Pete. *Red Moon Rising: How 24-7 Prayer Is Awakening a Generation*, Relevant Books, 2003, p. 119.

[5] This is paraphrased from *The Valley of Vision: A Collection of Puritan Prayers & Devotions*. Edited by Arthur Bennett, The Banner of Truth Trust, 1975, Introduction p. xv.

[6] Taylor, Charles. *A Secular Age*. First Harvard University Press, 2007, p. 302.

[7] Nietzsche, Friedrich. *The Gay Science.* (1882, 1887) para. 125. Edited by Walter Kaufmann, New York: Vintage, 1974, pp.181-82.

[8] Influenced by two works:

Taylor, Charles. *A Secular Age*. First Harvard University Press, 2007.

Smith, J.K. *You Are What You Love.* Baker Publishing Group, 2016.

[9] Plato. "The Allegory of the Cave". *The Republic,* Book VII.

[10] This thinking was informed by the work of J.K. Smith. *You Are What You Love.* Baker Publishing Group, 2016, p 19.

[11] Influenced by two works:

Taylor, Charles. *A Secular Age*. First Harvard University Press, 2007.

Smith, J.K. *You Are What You Love.* Baker Publishing Group, 2016.

[12] Influenced by the work of Cornelius Plantinga, Jr. *Not the Way it's Supposed to Be: A Breviary of Sin.* Eerdmans Pub. Co., 1995.

[13] *The Great Collection of the Lives of the Saints*. Volume 5, compiled by St. Demetrius of Rostov, Chrysostom Press, 2000.

[14] Excerpts from John 9 NLT

[15] Lewis, C.S. "The Silver Chair". *The Chronicles of Narnia,* First American Edition, Harper Collins, 2001, p. 633.

[16] Otto, Rudolph. *The Idea of the Holy*. Translated by John Harvey, First paperback edition, Oxford University Press, 1958, pp. 29-30.

[17] Otto, Rudolph. *The Idea of the Holy*. Translated by John Harvey, First paperback edition, Oxford University Press, 1958, pp. 6-7.

[18] Lewis, C.S. "The Lion, the Witch, and the Wardrobe". *The Chronicles of Narnia,* First American Edition, Harper Collins, 2001, p. 146.

[19] Exodus 3:14 NLT

[20] Matthew 16:15 NLT

[21] Paraphrased from Isaiah 52

[22] John 10:10

[23] Colossians 1:16

[24] John 20:11-19

[25] John 21

[26] Exodus 3

[27] Joshua 4

[28] Morrison, Van. "In The Garden". *No Guru, No Method, No Teacher,* Mercury Records, 1986.

[29] Job 12:10 NLT

[30] Psalm 19:1-4 NLT

[31] 1 Corinthians 10:31

[32] Romans 12:1 NLT

[33] Influenced by 1 Chronicles

[34] James 4:8 paraphrase

[35] Luke 6:45 NLT

[36] Bounds, E.M. *The Complete Collection of E. M. Bounds on Prayer.* Baker Books, 2004, p. 231.

[37] Klein, Laurie B. "I Love You, Lord". House of Mercy Music, 1978.

[38] "Act of Valor". Directed by Mike McCoy and Scott Waugh. Relativity Media, 2012.

[39] 2 Corinthians 5:17 NLT

[40] Luke 1:26-38 NLT

[41] Colossians 1:26 NLT

[42] Colossians 1:27 NLT

[43] referenced from Zechariah 4:6

[44] 2 Corinthians 3:18 NLT

[45] Luke 15:11-32

[46] Nouwen, Henri. *Return of the Prodigal Son.* First Image Books Edition, Double Day, 1994, p. 125.

[47] Chapin, Harry. "Cat's in the Cradle". *Verities and Balderdash*, Elektra Records, 1974.

[48] John 14:9 NLT

[49] John 14:20 NLT

[50] Romans 5:8 NLT

[51] Paraphrased from 1 Corinthians 13

[52] Romans 4:17 NLT

[53] Martin Jr., Bill and Eric Carle. *Brown Bear, Brown Bear, What Do You See?.* First board book edition, Henry Holt and Co., 1996, p. 1.

[54] Influenced by the work of Cornelius Plantinga, Jr. *Not the Way it's*

Supposed to Be: A Breviary of Sin. Eerdmans Pub. Co., 1995.

[55] Revelation 21:3-5 NLT

[56] Koyama, Kosuke. *Three Mile an Hour God*. SCM Press Ltd., 1979, p. 7.

[57] This general idea was sourced from the work of Richard Beck. *Unclean: Meditations on Purity, Hospitality, and Mortality.* Cascade Books, 2011.

[58] 1 John 4:18 NLT

[59] Matthew 11:19 NLT

[60] Mark 14

[61] Psalm 34:18 NLT

[62] Luke 7:14 NLT

[63] 2 Chronicles 20:12 NLT

[64] Plantinga, Jr., Cornelius. *Not the Way it's Supposed to Be: A Breviary of Sin.* Eerdmans Pub. Co., 1995, p. 10.

[65] Fujimura, Makoto. *Culture Care*. Fujimura Institute, 2015, p. 39.

[66] Matthew 6:10 NLT

[67] Paraphrase of 1 Corinthians 6:12

[68] There is no direct source for this quote, only stories of philosophers and tribal leaders saying it.

Zach Elliott describes himself as an ordinary man who loves Jesus. Anyone who knows Zach Elliott would describe him as far from ordinary. He is a church planter and a pastor from Oregon with a call to share the life and beauty of the gospel with the world. That calling carried Zach and his family to Tampa, Florida where he is pioneering a work to care for pastors and unite the church. He has a contagious love of life, finds beauty in the most unlikely places, and loves people with an uncommon depth of respect and honor.

www.zachjelliott.com

Rebecca Sandberg is a deep soul. Her profound love and respect for the human story informs her work as a writer, editor, artist, and speaker. Rebecca works with individuals, communities, schools, churches, and organizations to foster generative conversations, cultivate ideas, and grow relationships. Rebecca sees the world as a place of marvelous possibilities bringing awareness, clarity, and beauty to all of life and all that she does. Having spent many years living and working internationally, Rebecca founded Re:new Project, a nonprofit organization committed to employing refugee women from all over the world. Rebecca lives in the wine country of Newberg, Oregon with her husband and three young adult children.

www.rebecca-sandberg.com